Stylepedia

FASHIONARY

ISBN 978-988-13547-9-2
SN SPV102310PBCB

Designed and published in Hong Kong
by Fashionary International Ltd
Printed in China

Stylepedia is an ongoing project. If you have
any feedback, please don't hesitate to send it to
feedback@fashionary.org

🄵 @ fashionary
🄾 @ fashionary
🄿 @ fashionary

Fashionary Team 2023

A Visual Directory of Fashion Styles

Preface

STYLE, a blend of personal and cultural factors, is inseparable from fashion, its tangible canvas. They interact in a dynamic cycle, each influencing and being influenced by the other. This relationship reflects not only personal choices but also the wider world, from significant global events to the subtle vibe of local neighborhoods. Style and fashion are both products of their time and catalysts for change.

This book delves into the realm of style and fashion, examining how they shape and are shaped by the social, political and economic contexts in which they exist. It explores iconic styles and their origins and characteristics, tracing the threads that connect them to wider cultural narratives.

We hope you will find it an enlightening resource and a source of inspiration. You are also invited to bring your own perspectives and interpretations to this rich history, adding your voice to the diverse and vibrant tapestry of culture we all contribute to. This is not just a story about style and fashion, but a celebration of the many ways in which we express ourselves and make our mark on the world.

Great Depression (1929)

Jazz Age

The Modern

The early 20th century, a period of rapid modernization and social change, was marked by prosperity and optimism. Despite the economic hardship of the Great Depression, cultural milestones like the rise of jazz, women's suffrage, and the golden age of Hollywood offered glimmers of hope and innovation amid adversity.

19th Amendment (1920) – Women's suffrage in the United States

Era

Commercial radio broadcasting

Becky Sharp (1935) – The first feature-length color film

Flappers

Emerging in the 1920s, Flappers represented a bold, progressive attitude among young women. The name "flapper" refers to the flapping motion of their dresses while dancing, symbolizing a break from traditional norms.

An era of liberation

The Flapper movement emerged in response to societal changes after World War I and the women's suffrage movement. Seeking greater independence, women challenged traditional gender roles, adopting a more liberated lifestyle and a boyish look. The Prohibition era and the rise of jazz music further fueled the subculture, as young women frequented speakeasies and dance halls, embracing the excitement and defiance of the Roaring Twenties.

Dress code

Flappers often wore dropped waists and boxy-fit dresses with calf-revealing hemlines adorned with fringe, beads or sequins for evenings. They typically wore sheer stockings, Mary Janes or T-strap shoes and eye-catching costume jewelry.

❶ Cardigan & knit suit
A set included a long cardigan coat, drop-waist sweater, belt and pleated skirt. Mainly knitted, with woven trims such as satin, ensembles were boyish, comfortable and easy to put on.

❷ Headband
Often sparkling with rhinestone beads and paillettes or feathers.

❸ Cigarette holder
Protected the fingers, gloves and teeth from staining.

❹ Charleston dress
A short, loose, boxy dress that was sexy and allowed movement. The hemline usually had fringe, with sparkling beads, paillettes and embroidery in Art Deco patterns.

Long gloves

Drop-waist dress/skirt

Fringe

Eveningwear

Daywear

⑥ Cloche hat
Soft, close-fit, rounded hat. Women tucked their hair up inside the hat so it looked short.

⑥ Art Deco jewelry
Geometric, bold earrings, bracelets, necklaces and brooches.

⑦ Multiple faux-pearl strands
This signature Flapper look was popularized by Coco Chanel, who viewed jewelry as a fashion accessory rather than a display of wealth.

⑧ Purses
Purses, usually with straps, were highly decorative, with fringe and paillettes.

⑨ Feather boa/fan
These added glamour and sophistication to the Flapper look.

⑩ Mary Jane pumps
Worn for both day and evening, Mary Janes sometimes came in a T-strap style as well.

Torches of freedom
Flappers smoked to project an image of independence, liberation and sophistication as they displayed a rebellious spirit during an era of social change.

Hair & make-up
Flappers were known for their bold make-up, featuring dark lipstick, defined eyebrows and kohl-rimmed eyes. Their signature bobbed haircut was a short, sleek style that symbolized a break from traditional beauty standards.

Art Deco
Art Deco was a dominant aesthetic in the 1920s, and it heavily influenced Flapper fashion. It featured bold geometric shapes, symmetry and sweeping curves with exotic details.

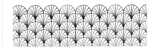

Rolled stockings & painted knees
Bare skin represented independence and modernity. Young Flappers often rolled down their stockings and used make-up to draw shapes on their bare knees, to draw attention as a rule-breaking act against traditional standards.

Lindy Hoppers

Named after aviator Charles Lindbergh, the Lindy Hop was a dance that emerged in the African-American community of Harlem, in New York City. It centered around an energetic swing dance that "hops" across the floor with acrobatic moves.

Jazz-fueled racial integration
Emerging at the height of the Harlem Renaissance, a period of African-American cultural and artistic expression, dancers developed the Lindy Hop by combining elements of jazz, tap and the Charleston as a means of self-expression and to escape the hardship of life. The dance played a significant role in furthering racial integration; the Lindy Hop was one of very few things that brought different races together to dance and socialize.

Dress code
Lindy Hoppers often wore loose-fitting and flashy clothes to allow freedom of movement —and to impress. Women wore patterned, fitted-waist swing dresses, while men donned suits or pants with suspenders and dress shirts. Both genders wore polished dance shoes.

Blouse

Fedora

V-neck sweater

Swing skirt

High-waisted wide-leg pants

Oxford shoes

Saddle shoes

🅕 Boutonniere/flower hairpin

Swingjugend

Swingjugend, German for "swing youth," was a counterculture movement that emerged in Nazi Germany during the 1930s. The name derived from their love of swing music, a genre banned by the Nazi regime for its "degenerate" American and Jewish influences.

Dance as resistance

The emergence of the *Swingjugend* was a response to the oppressive cultural policies of the Nazi regime. Swingjugend rejected Nazi ideology, instead embracing the freedom and individuality embodied by American swing music and adopting an elegant English style—both of which were deemed "un-German" by the Nazis. These rebellious middle- to upper-class youths cleverly employed music and attire as tools of defiance, hosting illicit parties and dancing to banned music, which served as both a bold assertion of their autonomy and an act of resistance.

Dress code

In contrast to the conservative Nazi style, Swingjugend style reflected the influence of American jazz and British tailoring. Men would wear long English jackets with wide-brimmed fedoras, while women would wear shorter skirts and dresses, heels and stockings.

Curled hair
A rejection of the Nazis' preference for braided hair.

Round sunglasses

Scarf

English-style jacket

Fedora

Trench coat

Baggy pleated pants

Pantyhose

Low-heeled shoes

⊕ English umbrella
Swingjugend carried umbrellas to look more English—regardless of the weather.

Depression-Era Elegance

The emergence of conservative and traditional fashion during the Great Depression provided people with a sense of normalcy in difficult times, maintaining a sense of dignity and style in the face of economic hardship.

Frugal yet stylish
The Great Depression brought a shift toward practicality and simplicity in fashion. Designers opted for elegant and sleek shapes over lavish embellishments, reflecting the changing social norms of the era. Versatile and cost-effective garments were created that were still aesthetically pleasing. The focus was on practicality, as women entered the workforce and needed functional and comfortable clothing that could be worn for multiple occasions.

Dress code
Depression-Era Elegance typically featured modest tailored clothing for both men and women. Women often wore feminine mid-calf to ankle-length dresses with fitted waists, while men donned suits with wide lapels and high-waisted, pleated pants.

❶ Tyrolean hat
A traditional Alpine hat made of felt or wool, featuring a brim and a distinctive corded band with a feather.

❷ Homburg/fedora
A key element, usually paired with a suit or overcoat.

❸ English drape
Suits featured a high waist and draped chest paired with fuller pants with a pleated front in a tapered shape, creating a relaxed fit that emphasized comfort and ease of movement.

Wide-leg
cuffed pants

Strapless
opera pumps

Fur-trimmed coat   Short gloves

4 Day dress
Day dresses featured a simple
silhouette for practicality and
comfort, with a fitted bodice and
slightly flared midi skirt. They were
made from lightweight fabrics
and adorned with ruffles and bows
to add a touch of femininity.

5 Sport coat
A tailored jacket made from wool
or tweed, worn for casual occasions
and outdoor activities; they usually
came in bold solid colors or plaids.

6 Wide belt
An important women's accessory
to be worn over a coat or jacket to
define the waist.

7 Oxford shoes
Women's Oxfords often came
with heels.

8 Pocket square
Its color usually coordinated with
a necktie.

9 Boater/newsboy cap
Both were summer hats worn
tilted to one side.

Marcel waves
Soft, feminine waves
were the key to the
style; Marcel waves
were particularly
popular.

Style icons
Prince Edward and Wallis Simpson were the style
power couple of the time, known for their impeccable
and sophisticated fashion sense. Edward favored
fine suits with wide lapels and bold patterns and
colors; Wallis wore classic streamlined dresses with
clean lines and statement jewelry.

Homemade clothes
The focus on simplicity and
resourcefulness led to
a rise in home dressmaking
and the use of patterns
from companies such as
Vogue and McCall's.

Hollywood Glam

Hailing from the 1930s, this style encapsulated the elegance, sophistication and allure of iconic movie stars during cinema's golden era, both on and off the silver screen.

Glamour as escapism

Hollywood Glam emerged during the Great Depression, providing a much-needed escape from harsh realities through lavish sets, luxurious costumes and larger-than-life stars like Greta Garbo, Jean Harlow and Clark Gable. The glamour and opulence of Hollywood legends became aspirational, leading to the widespread adoption of their fashion and aesthetic. The desire to emulate movie-star elegance and style provided an escape from daily struggles, and showcased the influence of Hollywood on popular culture.

Dress code

Hollywood Glam was characterized by bias-cut gowns made from shimmering and luxurious materials, often paired with fur stoles and sparkling jewelry.

❶ Puff sleeves
Usually seen on 1930s designs with fitted bodice and flared skirt. The puffs were made of lightweight fabric, creating a feminine and romantic look.

❷ Bias-cut gown
A long and lean silhouette, with fluidity and shimmery fabric cut on the bias, clinging to the body. Strapless designs were very popular in the 1940s.

Feather boa

Evening gown

③ Fur-trimmed coat
Fur was an important element in creating a luxurious image, sometimes dyed in bright colors for dramatic effect and worn by Hollywood stars on and off screen.

④ Opera gloves
Long, fitted gloves went over the elbow—sometimes even to the shoulders. They were often worn for formal occasions, for extra glamour.

⑤ Long silk scarf
This must-have accessory for women was often draped around the shoulders or neck.

⑥ "White on white" jewelry
Designers focused on creating highly sparkling jewelry for Hollywood stars on screen. Due to the nature of black-and-white movies in the 1930s, clear gems and white metal stood out better than colored gems.

⑦ Art Deco pumps
Featuring symmetric patterns and small perforations, the pumps were often made from metallic fabric or leather.

"Diamonds Are a Girl's Best Friend"
From the 1953 film *Gentlemen Prefer Blondes,* this Marilyn Monroe tune is the ultimate representation of the Hollywood Glam style.

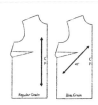

Bias cut
In this technique, pioneered by Madeleine Vionnet in the 1920s, a woven fabric is cut at a 45-degree angle to the grain. This allows the fabric to drape and stretch, creating a flowy and clingy fit.

Hair & make-up
Make-up featured bold, dramatic eyeliner and deep red lips, with arched eyebrows for a more expressive and alluring appearance. Hairstyles ranged from sleek finger waves to voluminous curls, creating an overall sense of refined and timeless sophistication.

Pachucos

This vibrant Mexican-American subculture emerged during the 1930s and 1940s in the United States. The name "Pachuco" is believed to have originated from the city of Pachuca, Hidalgo, in central Mexico.

¡Viva Mexico!

Pachuco subculture began in the early 20th century as Mexican immigrants sought to establish their identity in the United States. Many scholars believe it was a response to discrimination and a way to assert cultural pride. The Pachucos' distinctive style and behavior helped them stand out and defy societal norms. Key influences included jazz, swing and African-American culture, which contributed to the Pachucos' vibrant and rebellious spirit.

Dress code

The Pachuco style was characterized by zoot suits, which featured high-waisted, wide-leg pants and long jackets with padded shoulders. Accessories included wide-brimmed hats, flashy ties and long, dangling watch chains.

❶ Oversized fedora
Usually decorated with extra-large feathers.

Drape jacket

Short skirt

Fishnet stockings

Heeled sandals

Pachuca—
A female Pachuco

Extra-long pocket-watch chain

Skinny belt

Suspenders

Men's cardigan

Shirt

② Zoot suit
The oversized suit was a signature of Pachuco culture: an elongated drape jacket, pointed-collar shirt, and high-waisted baggy pants with pegged ankles.

③ Cross necklace
Pachucos often wore this symbol, which was related to their Mexican Catholic heritage.

④ Pocket watch
This accessory was often chained on a belt loop or lapel to keep it safe from pickpockets.

⑤ Two-tone dress shoes
Often two-tone wingtips would match the zoot suit's colors.

⑥ Swing tie
These are wide and often short, with bold geometric patterns or tropical brights.

Caló
Caló was a language adopted by Pachucos in the 1940s and 1950s. They wanted to create a culture that was uniquely their own, so they devised new words that combined Spanish and English.

Pachucos on the big screen
Actor Edward James Olmos portrayed a Pachuco in the 1981 movie *Zoot Suit*. The film is an adaptation of a play by Luis Valdez that tells the story of the 1940s Sleepy Lagoon murder trial and the subsequent Zoot Suit Riots in Los Angeles.

Hairstyle
Pachucos often styled their hair in pompadours or slicked-back looks, using generous amounts of pomade.

Zoot Suit Riots
The Zoot Suit Riots erupted in Los Angeles in 1943, fueled by tensions between Mexican-American zoot-suit wearers and white servicemen who saw the suits as unpatriotic due to the excess fabric working against the wartime effort of conserving resources.

Transforma
through Wa

World War II significantly reshaped fashion and style. The practical needs of wartime gave rise to new, functional trends, while the post-war period saw a surge in alternative subcultures and a return to luxury. The era left a lasting impact, fostering a future fashion landscape that was more casual, practical and diverse.

World War II (1939–45)

Casablanca (1942)

ion

The rise of synthetic textiles

Factory-made clothes

Rationed Fashion

World War II impacted not only global politics
and economies but also fashion. Despite
minor differences, many countries sought ways
to adapt to the challenges of war, developing
a simple yet practical style.

Respirator mask & bag
The UK government issued masks in
case of gas attacks. Special handbags
were designed to allow citizens to
carry them stylishly.

The queen's dressmaker
In 1942, a collection of "utility"
outfits designed by eight
designers—including Hardy
Amies and Norman Hartnell,
both of whom were official
dressmakers to Queen
Elizabeth II—was unveiled,
demonstrating attractiveness
under austerity.

"Make do and mend"
This UK government slogan
encouraged civilians to repair
and reuse their garments.

Tilt hat/doll hat

Siren suit

Two-
piece
skirt
suit

🇬🇧 UK

Wartime austerity fashion

Rationed fashion was a result of the scarcity of materials and restricted clothing production. Governments implemented rationing systems, limiting fabrics such as wool, silk and leather—often used for civilian clothing—for the war effort. Unnecessary fabric-consuming details were not allowed. Women wearing pants, overalls and military-inspired clothing also became more acceptable; since manpower was short, many women took over men's labor-intensive jobs, and even joined auxiliary services.

Dress code

Wartime clothing prioritized functionality and durability, such as simplified designs with minimal ornamentation, more form-fitting and military-like silhouettes, and shorter hemlines. Alternative materials, such as wood, rayon and cotton, were very common.

⊕ Liquid stockings
Since silk and nylon were rationed, women would paint their legs to mimic stockings.

Bandanna

Cotton shirtwaist dress

Bib overalls

Wooden wedges

Oxford heels

🇺🇸 **US**

Victory rolls
For this popular hairstyle, two rolls of hair were curled and pinned on top of the head. The V shape stood for victory.

Beauty as patriotic duty: Montezuma Red
The US government encouraged women to wear glamorous make-up to boost morale and go against Hitler's expectations of women. Lipstick and nail polish in a vibrant red known as Montezuma Red or Victory Red were issued by the military to match women's uniforms.

Pin-up Girls

Celebrating feminine beauty and glamour,
Pin-up style featured women in alluring, playful
poses. The term "pin-up" refers to pinning
the images to walls or locker doors.

Girls, girls, girls

Pin-up culture began in the
early 20th century, gaining
momentum during World War II.
Soldiers would carry pictures
of beautiful women as symbols
of idealized femininity and
reminders of what they were
fighting for. These images often
appeared in calendars and
magazines, and on the nose
art of military aircraft. The Pin-
up aesthetic was popularized
by artists such as Alberto
Vargas and Gil Elvgren, whose
illustrations depicted women with
hourglass figures in sensual
poses with playful expressions.

Dress code

The Pin-up style emphasized
sexiness without being excessive,
with fit-and-flare dresses,
high-waisted designs and
form-fitting tops accentuating
the hourglass figure. Bright
hues and playful patterns such
as polka dots added to the
fun, visually striking aesthetic.

❶ **Bathing suit**
Both one-piece suits and high-
waisted two-piece bikinis
were common in the '50s, creating
an hourglass silhouette.

❷ **Garter belt**
As a piece of lingerie that was
not supposed to be visible,
the garter belt was a classic element
of sexy teasing.

Halter dress

Strappy
heeled sandals

High-heeled shoes

High-waisted bikini

Off-shoulder top

High-waisted shorts

3 Sweetheart neckline
The low, curved style was used to accentuate the décolletage.

4 Wide-brimmed hat
The wide brim balanced out the new, slimmer silhouette of the late '40s.

5 Swing dress
The swing dress featured a fitted bodice and a full skirt that flared out from the waist. The style was often made from lightweight fabrics, and was perfect for twirling on the dance floor.

6 Cigarette pants/Capris
The high waist, flat-front silhouette and slim, tapered leg flattened the tummy and elongated the legs.

7 Pencil skirt
This tight-fitting skirt showed off the hips and was often worn with high-heeled pumps.

Nose art
During WWII, pin-ups were painted on the noses of warplanes. These illustrations of women in provocative poses were meant to boost morale.

Why seamed stockings?
Seamless stockings were not popularized until the 1960s; before that, seamed stockings were the only option. Modern Pin-up aficionados wear them as an homage to the original aesthetic; the back seam creates a long, smooth line and a touch of sexiness.

Hair & make-up
Pin-up hairstyles showcased classic glamour, with victory rolls and soft waves being popular choices. Make-up typically featured bold red lips, winged eyeliner and defined eyebrows.

Zazous

The Zazous were swing-loving French youths who stood against fascism with their distinctive style and passive resistance. The name comes from the refrain of the jazz song "Je Suis Swing."

Flamboyant French resistance
The Zazou movement was a reaction to the oppressive political climate and fascism during the 1940s. When the Vichy government began to rule France after the Nazi invasion, French youths' love of jazz, swing and flamboyant clothes was seen as distasteful, defiant and hostile to the conservative government. Their refusal to comply with its policies made them synonymous with freedom and resistance, and a target for suspicion and harassment.

Dress code
Zazous wore flamboyant styles, bright colors and bold patterns. Men wore drape suits resembling zoot suits, with long jackets and narrow, cuffed pants and colorful accessories. Women wore feminine silhouettes, with knee-length skirts and striped stockings or bobby socks.

Sunglasses

Bright red lipstick

Blonde curled hair
Women often went scarfless to show off their dye job.

Long, slicked hair

Collar pin

English umbrella

Bobby socks

Extra-long pocket-watch chain

Wooden platform shoes

Pegged pants

Passive defiance
The yellow Star of David was worn by Zazous as a fashion accessory, defying the intended humiliation and marginalization imposed by the Nazis on Jewish people.

Beats

The Beat movement emerged as a literary and cultural revolution led by writers, poets and intellectuals who rebelled against post-war social values. The term "Beat" symbolized being "beaten down" yet attaining an enlightened, "beatific" state.

Bohemian spirits awaken

The movement began in New York City as a reaction to the conservative, materialistic values of post-WWII society. Writers including Allen Ginsberg, Jack Kerouac and William S. Burroughs sought to break free from societal constraints and explore personal freedom through spirituality, sexuality and self-expression. Their work championed anti-establishment ideals and inspired future countercultural movements, including the hippies of the 1960s.

Dress code

Beats often wore casual and scruffy clothing, reflecting their anti-establishment attitude. Less fashionable workwear, such as crewneck sweatshirts, chambray work shirts, chinos and jeans were also wardrobe staples. Black, thick-framed and square-framed glasses became signature Beat styles.

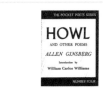

Howl (1956)

Ginsberg's poem is known for its raw, confessional style and unapologetic exploration of taboo themes.

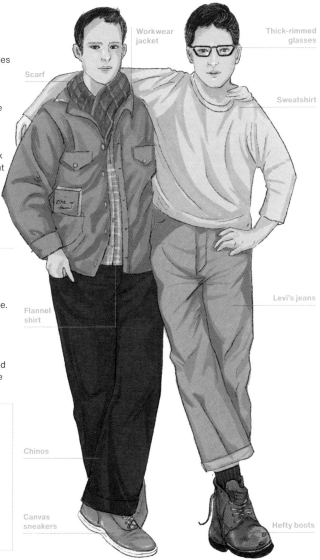

Workwear jacket

Thick-rimmed glasses

Scarf

Sweatshirt

Flannel shirt

Levi's jeans

Chinos

Canvas sneakers

Hefty boots

The New Look

The New Look, a collection by French couturier Christian Dior, was a fashion movement that emerged after WWII. It marked a departure from the austere fashions of the war years, emphasizing femininity, luxury and glamour.

The return of opulence
After WWII, the fashion industry sought to revitalize itself. In 1947, Christian Dior's "Corolle" collection, featuring ultra-feminine details like cinched waists, full skirts and padded hips, was dubbed the "New Look" by *Harper's Bazaar* editor Carmel Snow. The style symbolized a resurgence of luxury, femininity and opulence, and quickly gained popularity. The New Look defined the golden era of couture and marked fashion's revival as an art form and an expression of culture. It also represented a return to an optimistic and hopeful time.

Dress code
The ultra-feminine look emphasized dramatic silhouettes, with nipped-in waists, accentuated hips and voluminous skirts. Dresses were often made of heavy fabrics, such as silk taffeta and velvet, and featured feminine details including embroidery, bows and draping.

❶ Straw saucer hat
This conical straw hat was large and lampshade-like.

❷ Bar suit jacket
The iconic jacket of Dior's New Look featured round shoulders and a cinched waist; the hips were heavily padded for a rounded, hourglass shape.

❸ Peplum skirt
The hips were often draped with extra fabric for a voluminous effect, emphasizing fuller hips as well as responding to the bygone fabric-saving era.

Jolie Madame
by Pierre Balmain

New Look
by Christian Dior

4 Tailored jacket
Hourglass jackets featured round shoulders. One iconic example is the suit created by Hubert de Givenchy for actress Leslie Caron in 1955.

5 Billowy, full skirt
Usually worn over a petticoat for extra volume, full skirts were often paired with cropped jackets.

Pearl necklace

Top-handle bag

6 Feminine suit
Exquisitely tailored sets with feminine details, such as cinched waistlines and draped panels, were paired with sleek, slim skirts.

7 Gloves
Gloves bestowed the ultimate touch of feminine elegance.

8 Coordinated hat
Besides saucer hats, other hats, such as the capulet and pillbox hats, were popular.

9 High-heeled pumps
With spike heels and a streamlined shape.

10 New Look lingerie
Underwear with shaping functions, such as boning and laces, was ideal for creating the hourglass shape. These features helped enhance curves and create a flattering silhouette.

Sabrina (1954)
This classic romantic comedy revolves around the transformation of the titular character from a shy and awkward girl to a sophisticated and elegant woman, complete with a New Look style that exudes charm and grace.

Grace Kelly in *Rear Window*
The dress Kelly wore in the 1954 Hitchcock film, designed by Edith Head, became iconic.

Cristóbal Balenciaga
Balenciaga was known for his precision, his architectural shapes, and for using luxurious fabrics and bold colors. He was a major figure in the New Look movement, creating iconic alternative styles of the era, including baby-doll dresses and cocoon coats.

Hot Rodders

Derived from "hot roadster"—slang for a fast, customized car—Hot Rodders were a car-centered youth subculture in which young men would race their self-modified vehicles as an emotional outlet and a rebellion against conformity.

Revved-up rebels

Hot rodding was viewed as rebellious due to its potential danger and loud, disruptive nature. After WWII, surplus military equipment and affordable vehicles were widely available. Many mechanically skilled young veterans modified old cars by souping up engines and scrapping nonessentials in order to lighten the cars' weight. Soon, the media began to promote the culture to a wider teen audience; they were a new commercial demographic, aided by early hot-rod enthusiasts including Clay Smith and Ed Iskenderian, who self-marketed their expertise and innovations.

Dress code

A leather or wool bomber jacket featuring a car club's name, and a plain T-shirt or bowling shirt paired with cuffed jeans, was a signature Hot Rodder look. Aviator sunglasses were common, as were work boots and Converse sneakers.

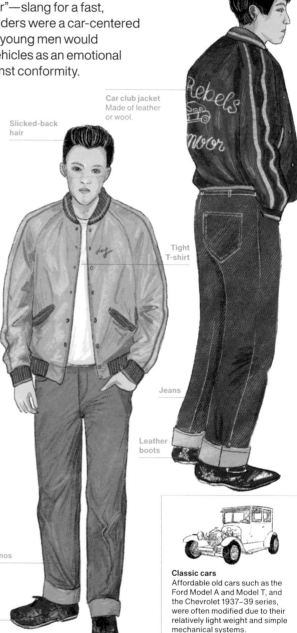

Slicked-back hair

Car club jacket
Made of leather or wool.

Tight T-shirt

Jeans

Leather boots

Chinos

Canvas sneakers

Classic cars

Affordable old cars such as the Ford Model A and Model T, and the Chevrolet 1937–39 series, were often modified due to their relatively light weight and simple mechanical systems.

Bills

Emerging in the late 1950s in Belgian Congo, the Bills were named after Buffalo Bill, an American cowboy figure who stood for individualism and freedom, which young Congolese yearned for. The Bills were characterized by a classic cowboy look.

The cowboy dream: liberation
As Congo was seeking independence from colonial rule, lower-class youth expressed their desire for liberation by dressing up as cowboys, which they saw as a symbol of freedom and victory. The Congolese were under the influence of Hollywood—especially the cowboy movies that were popular at the time. At some level, the cowboy craze was also an act of escape from the reality of economic hardship.

Dress code
Bills mimicked cowboy attire at a lower budget, wearing wide-brimmed hats, plaid shirts, sandals or leather boots, blue jeans and neckerchiefs. They also carried toy guns and homemade holsters.

⊕ Sandals
Since boots were not widely available, many Bills settled for sandals.

Cowboy hat

Neckerchief

Riding with Buffalo Bill (1954)

Homemade holster & toy gun

Pants/jeans

Cowboy boots

Outlaw Bikers

The Outlaw Biker subculture emerged in post-war California, deriving its name from "outlaw" motorcycle clubs—those not sanctioned by the American Motorcyclist Association (AMA).

Veterans & comrades

Outlaw Biker subculture started among former soldiers who found civilian life unbearable. They formed tight-knit motorcycle clubs that valued freedom and brotherhood over society's rules. These clubs established unique rules, ceremonies and hierarchy, distinguishing themselves from mainstream clubs. While most clubs were law-abiding, some clubs gradually became more lawless, engaging in organized crime and violence, solidifying their identity. This subculture has since spread globally, maintaining its distinct ethos and practices.

Sunglasses

Dress code

Outlaw Biker style incorporates military elements such as flight jackets and combat boots. They wear leather vests or jackets adorned with club patches, known as "colors." They typically favor jeans, boots and bandannas. Tattoos and jewelry, such as skull rings and chain wallets, are also common.

❶ Blue jeans
Jeans protect bikers from road rash and exhaust-pipe burns.

Heavy jewelry
The type of jewelry worn varies depending on the individual and the club. But it is typically heavy and masculine, with intricate metalwork.

Leather gloves
These protect the hands from friction and provide a better grip.

Tools/weapons
Tools or weapons hidden on a bike can be used for repairs or as a weapon if attacked.

1%er patch
This patch is worn to show one's Outlaw identity.

Bandanna
Bandannas keep sweat and oil off of the helmet's interior padding, and absorb dust.

Biker jacket
Also known as a "Perfecto," the classic biker jacket is a descendant of the A-2 military flight jacket. It is made of tough leather and has a diagonal zipper.

Cuts/cut-offs
"Cuts" are denim or leather jackets with the sleeves cut off. They are often decorated with club patches.

Engineer boots
Originally worn by the US Army Corps of Engineers, these durable boots provide traction and protection. They have no laces that could be hazardous on a motorcycle.

The Hollister Riot
After a motorcycle rally in Hollister, California, in 1947, a group of bikers caused a ruckus that made headlines. The name "1%er" came from the AMA's statement that these outlaws represented 1% of motorcyclists, and that the remaining 99% were law-abiding.

Outlaw ink
Tattoos are a prominent part of biker identity, with many members sporting club logos, skulls and other dark imagery. The tattoos reflect their rebellious ethos and serve as a means of expressing loyalty and individuality.

The Big Four
The most notable 1%er motorcycle clubs are the Hells Angels, the Outlaws, the Bandidos and the Pagans. The clubs are known for their outlaw status and involvement in criminal activity. They have a strong presence in the US and other countries.

Leathermen

The Leatherman subculture emerged in the post-World War II era, primarily among gay men who embraced a rugged, masculine aesthetic. The name "leatherman" stems from their preference for leather attire as a symbol of power and virility.

Biker jacket

Aviator sunglasses

Brotherhood among gay veterans

The subculture emerged as a reaction against rigid expressions of masculinity imposed on the gay community. Gay veterans of WWII bonded over their shared love of motorcycles and leather, creating a space where they could celebrate their sexuality openly and redefine masculinity on their own terms. The subculture had a significant influence on BDSM culture, with leather and bondage becoming key elements of BDSM fashion and aesthetics.

Dress code

Leathermen typically wear leather (or faux leather) pants, vests, chaps and jackets. Accessories like harnesses, cuffs, caps and boots are also common. The color black dominates the attire, signifying power, authority and eroticism.

Blue jeans

❶ Muir cap
This black cap is the signature accessory; it was popularized by the 1953 film *The Wild Ones* starring Marlon Brando.

Engineer boots

Tight leather pants

Dog collar

❷ Chaps
Often featured in Tom of Finland drawings, chaps are worn without pants underneath as a symbol of sex appeal and male liberation.

❸ Bandanna
These can be worn in any way, as long as the color is visible. Bandannas are often used to indicate the wearer's kink (see *The hanky code*).

❹ Body harness
The body harness is related to S&M sexual practices.

❺ Police shirt
Police or military uniforms are symbols of masculinity, reinforced by leather material.

❻ Gauntlets
Traditionally protective gear worn by cowboys and welders, gauntlets are a stark symbol of masculinity.

The hanky code
This non-verbal communication was used in gay subculture to indicate sexual preferences or fetishes; a colored hanky or bandanna was placed in a back pocket.

Color	Preference
Black	S&M/fetish
Dark Blue	Anal
Light Blue	Oral
Brown	Scat
Green	Hustler/prostitute
Grey	Bondage
Orange	Anything goes
Purple	Piercing
Red	Fisting
Yellow	Watersports

Tom of Finland
Tom of Finland's homoerotic drawings often feature stereotypically hyper-masculine working-class men such as sailors, soldiers and the like. His drawings are often associated with S&M.

Hairstyles
Military-inspired clean-cut or shaved heads, as well as beards and handlebar mustaches.

Why BDSM?
BDSM stands for bondage, discipline (or domination), sadism (or submission), masochism. Some practitioners engage in a strict hierarchy and code of protocol—similar to the military.

Tool Box Bar, 1963
Justin Hall's comic about the legendary Leatherman bar in San Francisco.

Seventeen magazine's first issue (1944)

Elvis Presley,
"Heartbreak Hotel" (1956)

Baby boom

James Dean, icon of teen rebellion

Post-war economic boom

Teen Power

Post-war prosperity birthed a distinct culture of teenagers, who were eager to differentiate themselves from their parents. Influenced by mass consumerism and entertainment, they began experimenting with fashion and subcultures as a form of rebellion and identity-seeking. This pivotal shift positioned teens as influential cultural catalysts, forever reshaping the landscapes of fashion and society.

Bobby Soxers

Emerging in the United States during the 1940s and 50s, Bobby Soxers were the earliest subculture consisting mainly of teenage girls. The name refers to their iconic ankle-length "bobby socks."

The rise of the teeny-bopper

During WWII, teenage girls in the US gained independence and freedom due to the lack of adult supervision, leading to a flourishing subculture fueled by popular culture. The rise of swing music, and artists such as Frank Sinatra, were key influences on the group. After the war, Bobby Soxers continued to symbolize teenage rebellion and self-expression, defining American youth culture and demonstrating the commercial power of teens.

Dress code

Characterized by casual schoolgirl fashion consisting of bobby socks, circle skirts, button-down blouses and crewneck sweaters, the style was accessorized with scarves and, occasionally, letterman jackets.

❶ Cuffed jeans
Rolled-up jeans with a black leather belt to hold them up.

❷ Circle skirt
These were mostly knee-length, and usually a solid color, but sometimes with checks or appliqués.

❸ Saddle shoes
Saddle shoes were often part of a school uniform, and could be dressed up or down.

Shetland sweater

Penny loafers

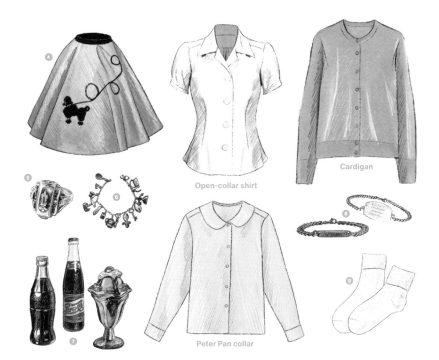

Open-collar shirt

Cardigan

Peter Pan collar

④ Poodle skirt
In 1947, singer Juli Lynne Charlot invented the poodle skirt as a last-minute Christmas party dress by cutting a circle out of a piece of felt and adding an appliqué.

⑤ Class-ring necklace
Some girls would wear their boyfriend's class ring on a chain.

⑥ Charm bracelet
Collecting charms for the bracelet was popular among young women.

⑦ Sodas & sundaes
Coca-Cola and Pepsi-Cola were popular during the 1940s; ice-cream sundaes were often sold in soda fountains.

⑧ Identification bracelet
Often stacked with other bracelets, ID bracelets were engraved with a name or initials.

⑨ Bobby socks
These ankle-length white cotton socks were first made in Britain to replace nylon stockings due to rationing.

"Swoonatra"
This term was coined to describe teenage girls' intense emotional response to Frank Sinatra's performances; they'd often scream and faint. Sinatra's good looks and "bad boy" persona made him an ideal object of infatuation.

Booze-free bars
Classic soda fountains were popular hangouts for Bobby Soxers. These establishments served soft drinks, ice cream and other treats.

Hairstyles
For rag curls, girls would tie strips of cloth in their hair in the evening, then brush it out in the morning, sometimes pinning it back with a barrette or headband.

Greasers

Named after their signature greased-back hairstyle, Greasers were a working-class youth subculture that emerged in the United States in the 1950s, with a cool, bad-boy look.

Grease is the word

Greaser subculture was a response to the economic boom and rise of consumerism after WWII. Greasers were mainly urban, working-class Italian-Americans and Mexican-Americans who were rejecting societal norms to forge their own identity. Inspired by rock 'n' roll and Hollywood actors like James Dean and Marlon Brando, they were known for loyalty to the group, a passion for fast cars and motorcycles, and a distinctive style featuring leather jackets and greased-back hair.

Dress code

Greasers' tough, streetwise image called for leather jackets, blue jeans, fitted T-shirts, and engineer boots or Converse sneakers. Women, also known as Greaser girls, often wore high-waisted skirts or tight pants along with scarves or bandannas.

❶ Fold-up jeans
Jeans were durable and affordable, and symbolized rebellion.

❷ Tight leather pants
Leather pants like those worn by the character Sandy Olsson in the 1978 film *Grease* were the epitome of bad-girl cool.

Fitted T-shirt

Black leather belt

Heels

Switchblade comb

Bandanna

Winston

Cigarettes

ROYAL CROWN HAIR DRESSING

Pomade

Sunglasses

❸ Leather jacket
The classic leather Perfecto biker jacket was made by Schott.

❹ Converse Chuck Taylor sneakers
Converse sneakers were comfortable and inexpensive; they were further popularized by James Dean.

❺ Engineer boots
These boots were popular among motorcyclists during the 1950s and '60s due to their rebellious image and their durability.

❻ Pedal pushers
Usually wore by women, pedal pushers were calf-length pants; today they're called capri pants.

❼ Pencil skirt
Pencil skirts, with their snug fit and high waistline, emphasized the curves of the female body, allowing women to express their femininity and sexuality.

❽ Sweetheart neckline
The low, curved neckline accentuated the bust and flattered women's silhouettes—this was a very desirable look during the 1950s and 1960s.

Diners & drive-ins
Greasers spent time hanging out at local diners, drive-ins and gas stations where they could show off their cars, bikes and fashion, and enjoy rock 'n' roll music.

Slicked-back hair
The pompadour, ducktail or jellyroll was the signature hairstyle, greased back with pomade or petroleum jelly.

Loud & powerful
Harley-Davidson motorcycles, especially the early Panhead, Knucklehead and Duo-Glide models from the 1940s and 1950s, were popular with Greaser subculture.

Grease (1978)
This musical romantic comedy vividly captured Greaser subculture through the character of Danny Zuko. John Travolta's portrayal embodied the movement's rebellious style and spirit.

Rockers

Rockers, also known as "Ton-up Boys," emerged in the 1950s in the United Kingdom. They were called Rockers due to their love of rock 'n' roll and fast motorcycles.

The wild ones

In response to the conservative values and societal norms of post-WWII Britain, young people sought freedom and individuality and gravitated toward American rock 'n' roll music and the motorcycle scene. Motorcycles were a more affordable mode of transportation than cars, allowing working-class youths to own a symbol of autonomy and defiance. Riding powerful bikes, gathering with friends, and listening to loud music provided an escape from the boredom and regimentation of post-war Britain, enabling young people to create their own identity and forge a new subculture.

Dress code

Rocker attire typically consisted of black leather jackets adorned with patches or studs; tight jeans; white or black T-shirts; and motorcycle boots. Accessories included bandannas, chains and fingerless gloves.

❶ Open-face helmet
Usually paired with aviator goggles—although some Rockers wore no helmet at all.

❷ Leather pants
Worn with matching jacket for a complete leather look and better protection.

❸ Motorcycle boots
Often made by Lewis Leathers or Goldtop. The design prevents laces getting caught on anything.

Aviator goggles

Blue jeans

④ Café racer
A sport motorbike with
non-essentials removed.

**⑤ Personalized leather
motorcycle jacket**
Heavily decorated with metal studs,
patches and badges of their favorite
bands, brands and motorcycle clubs.

⑥ Leather gloves
These provide a better grip and
more comfort on handlebars.

⑦ White silk scarf
Silk scarves were worn by
motorcyclists to keep out drafts and
prevent chafing from constant
head-turning.

⑧ Sea-boot socks
Worn by the RAF during WWII and
adopted by Rockers, these knee-high
socks kept feet warm and dry.

⑨ Brothel creepers
Rockers often wore brothel creepers
when not riding their motorbikes.

⑩ Badges & patches
Badges and patches reflected
interests and affiliations, such as
motorcycle clubs, military rank,
rock bands and other symbols of
rebellion and individuality.

Marlon Brando
Brando's portrayal of a
leather-clad motorcycle gang
leader in *The Wild One*
popularized the rebellious and
anti-authoritarian attitude.
His style became a hallmark
of Rocker subculture.

Ton-up Boys
Rockers' rebellious attitude and
love of speed inspired the term
"Ton-up Boys," referring to their
goal of "doing the ton"—reaching
100mph (approx. 160km/h)—
on their bikes.

Jukebox café racing
This term was coined to
describe high-speed
races between cafés. The
racers would start when
they heard a certain song
playing on the jukebox,
the goal being to reach
the next café before their
rivals. Since the songs
typically lasted around two
minutes, the races required
superior driving skills and
high-performance bikes.

Teddy Boys

Originating in Britain, Teddy Boy subculture gained attention for its distinctive fashion and defiant attitude. The term "Teddy" was derived from the word "Edwardian," reflecting the influence of Edwardian-era clothing on their style.

Defiance through Edwardian style

The Teddy Boy movement originated as a working-class response to austerity in post-World War II Britain. Savile Row tailors created the Edwardian suit style to revive fashion from the post-war doldrums; the style was then adopted by young working-class people. Mixing this look with inspiration from American movies and rock 'n' roll music, Teds developed a unique fashion that combined elements of Edwardian style with modern cuts. Their rebellious attitude and fashion choices made them stand out; they quickly gained popularity among disaffected youth.

Dress code

The style is known for its fusion of highly stylized Edwardian fashion with an American rock 'n' roll/Western touch. Teddy Boys aimed for an exaggerated, flashy look; Teddy girls adopted masculine-style suits or skirts and espadrilles.

❶ Single-breasted jacket
This must-have item usually had a velvet collar.

❷ Slim Jim tie
A skinny tie was an essential part of a Teddy Boy look—usually with a Windsor knot.

❸ Colorful socks
Socks sometimes coordinated with drape suits, and came in loud colors.

❹ Drainpipe pants
These narrow and short pants show off the wearer's socks.

Silk scarf

High-collar shirt

Ballet flats

Judy—A female Teddy Boy

Coolie hat

Clutch bag

Bootlace tie

Pencil skirt

Brothel creepers

Espadrilles

Drape suit

⑤ Rolled-up jeans
High-waist, rolled-up, mid-calf-length jeans were adopted from American Rocker girls.

⑥ Maverick tie
This American Western style of tie was influenced by Hollywood cowboy movies.

⑦ Cameo brooches
These were usually worn by Judies with a white shirt or a Maverick tie.

⑧ Flick knife
Also known as switchblades, flick knives were used in gang fights.

⑨ Brocade vest
Vests were often made from silk or other expensive fabric, with rich patterns.

⑩ Drape suit
The Edwardian drape jacket was long, and had velvet trim on the collar and cuffs.

Notting Hill race riots
In 1958, Teddy Boys attacked the homes of West Indian residents for more than a week. Teds were hostile toward immigrants who had been recruited by the UK government to help rebuild the country. The riot solidified the Teddy Boy subculture's violent reputation.

Jive dancing
An energetic, acrobatic form of jive—the upbeat tempo of rock 'n' roll music—influenced the Teddy Boy style with its frenzied energy, duck walks, spins and flips.

The ducktail
The signature style, slicked-back hair on the back and sides, featured a longer, voluminous top that was combed upwards and back. The front of the hair often formed a wave-like shape.

QUADROPHENIA

***Quadrophenia* (1979)**
This film depicted Mod-vs-Rocker rivalry and violence, capturing the tribal nature of the two subcultures.

Ivy Leaguers

Ivy League universities are the most prestigious educational institutions in the United States. The iconic clothing style reflects the sophistication and elite status associated with these schools.

Quintessential campus style

Emerging in the early 20th century, Ivy League style was a unique dress code for the students of these distinguished universities. The look set itself apart from traditional attire by incorporating elements of British tailoring and American sportswear, emphasizing upper-class leisure and privilege. The style gained widespread popularity in the 1950s and has continued to transcend generations and regions. Its timeless and effortless sophistication have resonated with diverse audiences and multiple subcultures.

Dress code

Signature elements include tailored blazers, Oxford shirts, chinos and classic knitwear. Patterns such as tartan, argyle and stripes are also common. The look is often complemented with carefully chosen accessories including ties and leather belts.

❶ Sport coat
Two or three buttons at the cuff; flap or patch pockets; suede elbow patches. Usually tweed or herringbone fabric.

Harvard clip
Short, slicked-back hair on the sides, and a small pompadour.

Club tie

Navy blue blazer

Argyle sweater vest

Earth-tone chinos

Bermuda shorts

Penny loafers

② Sack suit
The name "sack suit" comes from the idea that the jacket hangs loosely and resembles a "sack" or a sweater. The suit is known for its casual, relaxed fit, with minimal padding and a boxy silhouette.

③ Bicycle
Bicycles are a popular mode of transportation for college students who want to get around campus easily.

Cashmere twinset

Argyle socks

Knitted tie

④ Regatta club blazer
Also known as rowing blazers, regatta blazers originated at Oxford and Cambridge universities. The brightly colored blazers feature contrast piping and patterns denoting the club.

⑤ Cricket sweater
These are usually a cable-knit pattern.

⑥ Oxford cloth button-down shirt
Originally a sportswear item worn in polo games, the shirt is now a classic, no-fuss staple that can be worn formally or informally.

⑦ Letterman sweater
Also known as a varsity sweater, a letterman sweater features an oversized letter (an H for Harvard, for instance) and is given to a member of a sports team.

Competitive sports
Ivy League schools are known for their competitive athletics programs, particularly rowing. Members of this elite group often enjoy other prestigious outdoor activities such as sailing and polo.

Penn   COLUMBIA   HARVARD   Dartmouth   Yale   Cornell   BROWN   PRINCETON

The Ivy League
The Ivy League comprises eight elite American universities, and connotes academic excellence, selectivity in admissions, old money and social elitism.

Vassar girls
Vassar was a prestigious college for women (it became co-ed in 1969). The stereotypical "Vassar girl" was privileged, intellectual and socially progressive. Their sophisticated look shared elements of Ivy League style, emphasizing intellect and status.

Miyuki-zoku

Miyuki-zoku was named after Miyuki Street, in the Ginza district of Tokyo. Its adherents embraced Western fashion and music, creating a style that still inspires Japanese fashion today.

Western-inspired Japanese youth

Miyuki-zoku subculture emerged as a response to changing social and cultural norms. Blending American Ivy League and British Mod fashions, young people created a unique style that symbolized rebellion against traditional Japanese norms and reflected the growing influence of Western culture. Its adoption of jazz music, and its blending of styles, demonstrated an eagerness to embrace global trends and establish a cosmopolitan identity that reflected a desire for a more progressive and open society.

Dress code

The look was sophisticated and polished, with a nod to American Ivy League style, including tailored suits, skinny ties and penny loafers. Women wore short skirts, high heels and bouffant hairstyles.

White button-down shirt

Dark, skinny tie

3-roll-2 blazer

Khaki chinos/ black pants

Penny loafers

Letterman sweater

Madras pants

White canvas sneakers

Say no to *Gakuran*
Gakuran is a traditional Japanese boys' school uniform, characterized by a stand-up collar and brass buttons.

The Code of the Striped Tie

Since 19th-century Britain, the striped tie has been a display of group identity. The variations in stripe thickness, direction and color are unique to each school, club or military regiment.

❶ Club ties

With their origins in 19th-century private clubs in England, club ties feature distinct—often diagonal—stripes or emblems. The designs represent a club's heritage, fostering a sense of belonging among members.

❷ University ties

In both Britain and the US, university ties display school colors, crests or symbols. They serve as an emblem of educational institution affiliation, promoting unity among students and alumni, and highlighting academic pride.

❸ Regimental ties

Following British military tradition, regimental ties showcase colors, patterns and emblems reflecting a unit's unique history and identity. They're typically worn by serving members, veterans and their associates, symbolizing respect and remembrance for their service.

The origins of the tie

The necktie traces its origins back to a Croatian military regiment of the 17th century that sported cravats. This unique neckwear intrigued Louis XIV of France, who adopted the style, sparking a widespread fashion trend.

In the US, club tie stripes run from the right shoulder to the left hip. When Brooks Brothers introduced repp ties to the US, they cut them in this direction to differentiate them from their British counterparts.

In the UK, regimental tie stripes run from the left shoulder to the right hip— "from heart to sword."

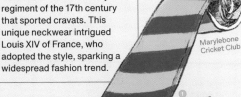

Marylebone Cricket Club ❶

London School of Economics

Oxford University, Jesus College ❷

Royal Dragoon Guards

Royal Navy

Parachute Regiment ❸

James Bond wears a Royal Navy tie

What is repp?

Repp is ribbed woven fabric that contains tiny, palpable wales or ridges. Repp ties can be distinguished from other striped ties by the fabric's texture.

Stilyagi

Meaning "style hunter" in Russian, *Stilyagi* was characterized by flamboyant Western-inspired fashion and a love of American culture, which was taboo at the time.

The call of the West

The *Stilyagi* subculture was a reaction to Soviet repression and dictatorship. After the increased exchange with Western allies during WWII, young Russians found American music, fashion and movies fascinating. In the 1950s, the Soviet government had strict rules about modest and conformist fashion. Stilyagi challenged those rules by imitating zoot suiters and Teddy Boys, and dancing to jazz and rock 'n' roll, in order to express their individuality and desire for a vibrant and open society.

Dress code

The Stilyagi dress code was characterized by bright colors, bold patterns and eclectic combinations. This included loud shirts, ties and jackets with tight, cropped pants for men, while women wore voluminous skirts and heeled sandals paired with statement jewelry.

Bright-colored suit jacket

Palm-tree tie
Hand-painted with American imagery

Statement jewelry

American-style dress

Cropped pants

Modest Soviet clothing

Thick-soled shoes

Souls for sale
Soviet propaganda often illustrated Stilyagis' embrace of Western culture as degenerate.

Raggare

Derived from the Swedish verb *ragga*, which means "to pick up girls," *Raggare* are working-class young people who are fascinated by American culture, movies and lifestyle.

American car craze

After WWII, Swedish working-class youths were able to afford cars. They were captivated by rebellious American Hot Rod culture, rock 'n' roll and Greasers. As post-war Sweden was still a conservative society, young people longed for freedom and independence from the previous generations. They preferred big, loud cars that symbolized the American dream and would differentiate them from the middle class. As American cars were not yet widely available, they were highly sought after.

Dress code

Raggare adopted an American working-class dress style— a typical Greaser look featuring a leather jacket, white T-shirt, jeans and a large pompadour. Women often dressed like Pin-up Girls in polka-dot dresses, capri pants, neckerchiefs and rolled hair.

Pompadour hairstyle
Borrowed from American Greasers.

Rolled hair

Bomber jacket

Fitted blouse

Straight-fit jeans

Capri pants
Inspired by Pin-up style.

Biker boots

Raggarbrudar—
A female Raggare

Cruising
Raggare cruise around to showcase their cars and socialize with each other while picking up girls; there is also often music and dancing.

Beatniks

A post-WWII cultural phenomenon, Beatniks derived their name from the slang term "beat," signaling their rebellion against traditional values. Their ethos was characterized by a detachment from society and an embrace of artistic self-expression.

The Beat ethos

The Beatnik subculture sprouted in the late 1950s. They were often seen as adherents or imitators of the Beat Generation. Coined by Herb Caen, a *San Francisco Chronicle* columnist, the term "Beatnik" often referred to a stereotype that superficially adopted Beats' mannerisms. Beatniks were typically younger followers who caricatured the anti-establishment ethos of the Beats with more eccentric nonconformist behavior. They embraced a bohemian lifestyle, celebrating art, jazz, poetry and Eastern spirituality while rejecting mainstream values and materialism.

Dress code

Beatnik style emulated French bohemian artists and jazz musicians. They favored a casual style of dress, often wearing black turtleneck sweaters, berets and dark sunglasses.

❶ Black turtleneck
This signature item was often worn fitted. It was a simple, unisex piece that was both understated and recognizable, embodying the Beatnik rejection of excessive patterns or colors.

❷ Breton stripes
Another nod to French fashion, Breton stripes were also popular. The simple design was unisex and lent a hint of pattern without being too flashy.

Cigarette pants

Loafers

A-line skirt

Bongos

Horn-rimmed glasses

Black leotard

Rolled-up jeans

Bateau neckline

③ Ballet flats
Women often wore ballet flats, choosing comfort over the high heels that were the standard for women at the time.

④ Black tights
Typically opaque and paired with a skirt, tights helped create an all-black look.

⑤ Beret
Inspired by French intellectuals and artists, berets were a popular accessory. They added an artistic, intellectual touch to the overall look. The iconic hat was also worn by Dizzy Gillespie.

Audrey Hepburn as a Beatnik
In the 1957 film *Funny Face*, Hepburn's character transforms from a demure bookshop clerk into a Beatnik-inspired fashion model. Her look featured a black turtleneck, capri pants and a beret.

Dizzy Gillespie
Gillespie was a prominent jazz musician whose innovative contributions to the genre had a significant influence on the Beatniks and their countercultural attitudes. His bebop music, characterized by its complex rhythms and improvisational style, resonated with the Beatniks' desire for self-expression and authenticity.

Beatnik slang
The Beatniks had their own unique slang and language. They remain a part of popular culture today.

"Cool"	Stylish or impressive
"Dig it"	To understand or appreciate something
"Square"	Conformist or uncool
"Hip"	Fashionable or in the know
"Chick"	A cool woman
"Cat"	A cool man

Hairstyles
The typical Beatnik hairstyle for men was long and shaggy, while women wore long, lank locks, conveying their disdain for a more conventional polished look.

Cuban missile crisis (1962)

Beatlemania

The Swingi.

The 1960s were a youth-centric era of optimism driven by technological advancements and economic prosperity. Art and fashion mirrored this daring and playful spirit, serving as significant reflections of this dynamic era. Concurrently, the surge in well-educated youth emerged as a transformative societal force. Their heightened social conscience paved the way for significant political movements.

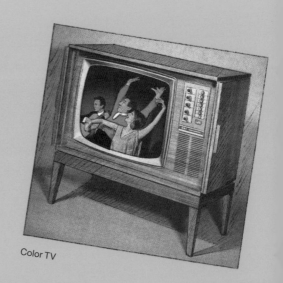

Color TV

Apollo 11 mission (1969)

g Sixties

Star Trek (1966)

Pop Art movement

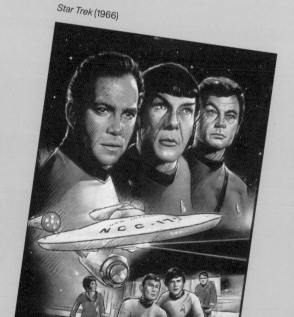

Mods

Mod subculture captivated young people with its unique blend of fashion, lifestyle and music. The name was derived from "modernist," reflecting Mods' love of contemporary trends.

Young, modern & free

Born from a desire for change and individuality, the Mod movement combined African-American R&B, British beats and Jamaican ska influences with Pop Art-inspired visuals. Young people, stifled by post-war conservatism, embraced cutting-edge fashion influenced by Italian and French styles. The Mods' fashion-forward spirit and love of underground clubs offered an escape from working-class life, reflecting the era's socioeconomic climate and a hunger for self-expression.

Dress code

Mod fashion was sharp and tailored, with an emphasis on clean lines and bold colors. Men donned slim-fitting cropped suits and narrow ties, while women opted for A-line dresses and mini skirts. Accessories such as large jewelry and Italian scooters completed the look.

❶ Bold prints
Pop Art influenced fashion with bold colors and graphic patterns.

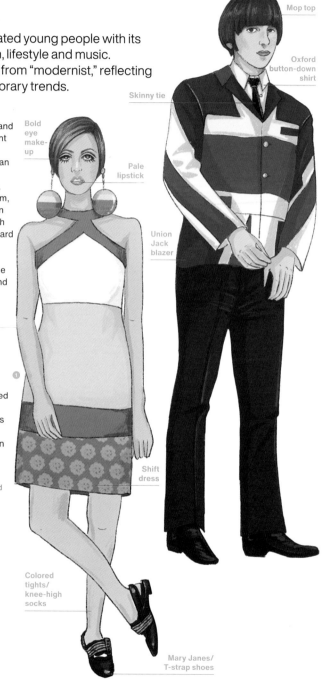

Mop top

Oxford button-down shirt

Skinny tie

Bold eye make-up

Pale lipstick

Union Jack blazer

Shift dress

Colored tights/ knee-high socks

Mary Janes/ T-strap shoes

Ankle boots

② Slim-fit cropped suit
Suits were clean and streamlined, slim and slightly cropped, with narrow lapels and often in a single-breasted style. Pants were usually tapered and had a flat front.

③ Mini skirt
Skirts became progressively shorter from the early 1960s, worn 6" to 7" above the knees.

④ Italian scooter
Italian scooters, usually Vespas or Lambrettas, were prized for their stylish designs, which complemented the Mod aesthetic.

⑤ A-line coat
A continuation of the elegant Jackie O style, A-line coats came in eye-popping colors and a minimalist design.

⑥ Large accessories
Under the influences of Pop Art and technology, resin, vinyl and Perspex were mass-produced into large, colorful, affordable accessories.

⑦ Chelsea boots
These short boots with Cuban heels and pointed toes were often worn by the Beatles.

⑧ Royal Air Force roundels
This target was originally painted on WWI British planes, and became an iconic Pop Art Mod symbol.

Secrets of the Internal Combustion Engine (1967), by Eduardo Paolozzi

Pop-Art influence
Pop Art inspired the use of bold colors, graphic designs, synthetic materials and humor. The crossover between Pop Art and fashion blurred the lines between fine art and popular culture.

Why all the mirrors and lights?
Mods sometimes decorated their scooters with an excessive number of mirrors and lights as a form of personal expression and to mock the law, which required at least one rear-view mirror fitted on the vehicle.

Biba
This London store epitomized the Mod aesthetic of the 1960s and 1970s. Biba created designs that were affordable and accessible, and reflected a youthful, playful spirit.

Space Age

Inspired by the fascination with space exploration, the Space Age subculture reflected the influence of the era's technological advancements and the race to conquer the cosmos.

The sky's the limit
In the 1960s, a sense of optimism and fascination with the future inspired a new aesthetic in fashion and design. Rapid technological advancements and the "space race" between the US and the Soviet Union fueled the imagination of designers and artists, leading to the exploration of new materials and designs that celebrated progress. This futuristic aesthetic embraced visions of space travel and reflected the excitement and possibility of the time.

Dress code
Innovative fabrics like PVC, metallics and synthetics echoed the aesthetics of astronauts and spacecraft. Designs incorporated geometric shapes, bold colors and streamlined silhouettes, showcasing a futuristic and optimistic view of what fashion could become.

❶ **Helmet hat**
Headwear was inspired by astronauts' helmets.

❷ **Go-go boots**
White knee-high or ankle-length go-go boots were popularized by fashion icons like Twiggy and Nancy Sinatra. They were often paired with short skirts or dresses.

Chain-mail design

Glossy gloves

A-line skirt/ dress

Space Age
television

Long patent leather boots

❸ Chain-mail dress
The iconic chain-mail dress designed by Paco Rabanne was made from plastic or metal geometric pieces instead of fabric.

❹ Gloves
Gloves were often made from synthetic metallic materials including silver vinyl or PVC that matched boots or other accessories.

❺ Futuristic coat
Coat styles featured minimalist silhouettes, bold colors and innovative materials. Unusual details like oversized buttons and asymmetrical panels added to the edgy look.

❻ Cutout A-line dress
Futuristic and avant-garde dresses often featured shiny or metallic fabrics, geometric shapes, high necklines and bold colors.

❼ Eskimo sunglasses
The plastic frames designed by André Courrèges were inspired by traditional Inuit snow goggles.

Helmet designed by Emilio Pucci for Braniff Airways.

Futuristic hair
Sleek bobs and voluminous hairstyles were often adorned with hairpieces, further accentuating the subculture's otherworldly aesthetic.

The 1963 Ball Chair, designed by Eero Aarnio.

Sputnik
The launch of *Sputnik* by the Soviet Union in 1957 marked the beginning of the Space Age, and sparked a new interest in space travel and technology.

The Cosmocorps collection by Pierre Cardin.

Iconic designers
Pierre Cardin, André Courrèges and Paco Rabanne played a major role in shaping the Space Age aesthetic. Cosmocorps (Cardin) and Moon Girl (Courrèges) are regarded as iconic Space Age collections.

Cosmos-inspired interiors
Architecture and interior design during this period were heavily influenced by the Space Age aesthetic. Decor incorporated shiny metals, spherical shapes, and ultra-modern designs.

Jackie O

This timeless fashion trend is named after former first lady Jacqueline Kennedy Onassis. Her iconic style is characterized by an elegance, sophistication and simplicity that continues to inspire modern fashion.

The first lady of style

Jackie Kennedy became a symbol of American elegance during her time as first lady. Her fashion choices, often inspired by French couture, and created by American designer Oleg Cassini, were a symbol of refinement and grace. The public admired her effortless poise and chic ensembles, which quickly became a significant influence on fashion trends. Women across America—and beyond—emulated her style, coveting the sophisticated and polished look that became synonymous with Jackie O.

Dress code

Jackie O's style emphasized quality fabrics, clean lines and understated elegance rather than flashy or embellished items. Simple A-line shapes, solid colors and clean lines created an effortlessly polished look.

❶ Boxy jacket/suit
Cropped at the waist, and with three-quarter sleeves, the jacket could be paired with a matching pencil skirt—the classic Jackie O way.

❷ Gloves
Often paired with an elegant suit or couture, white gloves have symbolized purity and nobility for centuries.

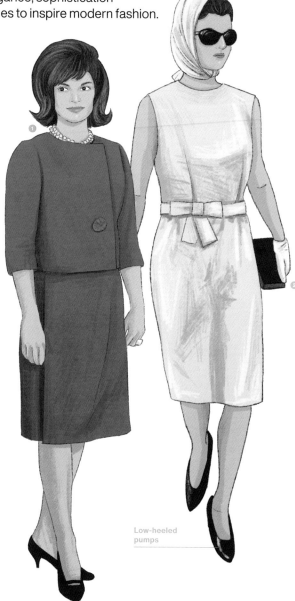

Low-heeled pumps

Top-handle handbag

Ballet flats

Oversized sunglasses

③ Sheath dress
Form-fitting from the bodice to
the hem, sheath dresses emphasize
an hourglass figure. They often
feature a slit to facilitate movement.

④ Trapeze coat
A simple color-block coat with
either no collar or a Peter Pan collar,
large buttons and no decoration.

⑤ Trench coat
This relatively casual staple of
Jackie's wardrobe was often worn with
a shift dress or a blouse and pants.

⑥ Silk scarf
Jackie's scarf was usually wrapped
around her head and paired with
oversized sunglasses.

⑦ Pillbox hat
This signature accessory often
matched the color of the outfit. It was
worn at an angle, tilted slightly to
one side.

⑧ Pearl necklace
A three-strand pearl necklace is the
most classic example.

"I want them to see what they've
done to Jack."

The pink suit
One of the most iconic pieces of
clothing associated with Jackie O's style
is the pink Chanel suit she wore on the
day of her husband's assassination.
The classic wool bouclé suit has become
a symbol of Jackie O's elegance and
grace under pressure.

Gucci Jackie bag
Jackie O's love of her Gucci bag
helped make it one of the most
sought-after accessories of the
1960s and 1970s. With its timeless
and practical design, the bag has
become synonymous with her
classic style.

Bouffant hair
A voluminous,
shoulder-length style with
soft, voluminous waves.

Surfers

Surfer style was the product of surfing subculture in California and Hawaii. The lifestyle emphasized sun, sand and riding ocean swells on surfboards.

The search for endless summer
Surfing can be traced back to ancient Polynesian cultures, but it was in the 1960s that the Surfer subculture truly flourished. Amid the Cold War and rising social tensions, the laid-back lifestyle of surfers offered an appealing escape. The Beach Boys' music, along with the counterculture movement, attracted young people to the West Coast, where they sought freedom and rebellion. Surfing competitions, surfboard innovations, and films like the 1966 documentary *The Endless Summer* further popularized the sport and solidified the Surfer image as a symbol of alternative living.

Dress code
Surfers in the 1960s embraced a casual, beach-ready style. Men wore board shorts and light clothing, while women favored bikinis and one-piece swimsuits with vibrant colors and patterns. Many sported bleached blonde hair from constant sun exposure.

❶ Bikini
Bikinis were often brightly colored, featuring bold patterns and prints that reflected the vibrant, free-spirited surf culture.

❷ Henley shirt
This popular 1960s style was collarless, with a placket in the front. Various bright colors were available, often with stripes.

Suntanned skin

Hawaiian shirt

Sweatshirt

One-piece swimsuit

❸ Longboard
In the 1960s, the longboard was the dominant surfboard; it was typically made of wood or foam and fiberglass.

❹ Board shorts
Board shorts featured bold colors, patterns and prints ranging from florals to psychedelic swirls, with unique design details such as decorative ties or lace-up fronts.

❺ Woodie
This classic '60s surfmobile was a station wagon with wooden panels on the sides and back. It had plenty of room for surfers to carry multiple longboards to the beach.

"Locals only"
Since good surfing spots are seasonal and rare, territoriality would arise among surfers who wanted to guard certain places; they sometimes resorted to verbal or physical threats, shouting "locals only!" at outsiders.

The Beach Boys
Heavily influenced by the surfing scene in the 1960s, the Beach Boys were hugely successful and influential; they are widely credited for popularizing surf rock.

Gidget (1959)
Gidget ignited a fascination with surf culture in the 1960s, popularizing the carefree, sun-soaked lifestyle. The film introduced a wider audience to surfing, transforming it from a niche pastime into a mainstream sport. Its impact rippled throughout fashion, music and youth culture.

Skinheads

Forming in the United Kingdom, this distinct youth movement captured the attention of society, and was characterized by its working-class ethos. The name refers to their close-cropped hair, which stood in stark contrast to the long hair that was popular at the time.

Unity through style

The UK Skinhead subculture emerged from working-class neighborhoods and drew inspiration from Jamaican Rudeboy culture and British Mod fashion. Disillusioned by Hippies' focus on peace, love and individualism, Skinheads fostered values of patriotism, hard work and loyalty, projecting a tough, masculine image to emphasize resilience in the face of economic hardship. Flourishing in the 1970s, the movement became associated with extremist political ideologies, leading to misunderstandings and negative stereotypes.

Dress code

Skinhead style combines elements of Mod and Rudeboy styles, and features slim-fitting jeans or pants, button-down shirts, skinny suspenders and Dr. Martens boots. Harrington jackets, bomber jackets, and Fred Perry polo shirts are also common staples.

① MA-1 bomber jacket
Originally a US Air Force jacket worn by pilots in the 1950s and 1960s, MA-1s were later donated to thrift stores. From there, they became an affordable clothing option.

② Fishnet tights
Influenced by Punk culture, Skinhead girls often wore fishnets with mini skirts.

③ Combat boots
Dr. Martens boots were a popular choice due to their comfort and durability.

Close-cropped/ shaved hair

Button-down shirt

Denim jacket

Mini skirt

Rolled-up jeans

White socks

Dr. Martens

Skinbyrd—A female skinhead

Checked shirt

Crombie coat

Union Jack top

Suspenders are a more affordable and comfortable option than belts, and were widely adopted by Skinheads.

⑤ Polo shirt
Fred Perry was the iconic polo-shirt brand. While it was associated with tennis, an upper-class sport, it was affordable to working-class kids.

⑧ Donkey coat
This heavy work coat was typically worn by the British working class. It was made from thick wool and came in navy, black or dark gray.

⑦ Pins & badges
Pins and badges featuring bands, football-team logos, etc. often adorned denim and bomber jackets.

Sharps
While some Skinheads are affiliated with far-right ideologies, many identify as apolitical or left-wing. The late 1970s saw the emergence of SHARPs (Skinheads Against Racial Prejudice), who advocated racial equality and anti-racism.

Chelsea cut
This hairstyle, popular among female skinheads, features long bangs and a shaved back and sides, often with a small tail.

Football fever
Many Skinheads passionately support their local football team. This enthusiasm has sometimes spilled over into hooliganism and violent clashes between rival fans, further fueling the subculture's tough, aggressive image.

Musical influences
Jamaican ska, reggae, and British rocksteady resonated with Skinheads' working-class background. They later incorporated Punk and Oi! music, which reflected their rebellious spirit with blue-collar themes and singalong choruses.

Suedeheads

An offshoot of the Skinhead movement, Suedeheads had slightly longer hair than their predecessors—as well as a dressier clothing style.

The dressier heirs of British toughs

Suedeheads were more moderate than Skinheads, seeking a sense of community and responding to the changing social and political landscape. They were generally apolitical and inclusive, as they adopted the liberal and civil-rights values of the decade. To distance themselves from their aggressive and far-right predecessors—while maintaining affinity for their working-class roots—Suedeheads opted for a more polished and sophisticated look, and drew inspiration from Mod, Ivy League and early Glam Rock fashions.

Dress code

Suedeheads incorporated British tailored elements into their tough workwear. Tonic suits and button-down shirts were paired with slim or straight jeans, Crombie coats or Harrington jackets. Polished shoes like brogues and loafers were signature items for both genders.

Smoothies
Some Suedeheads grew their hair to their shoulders, becoming what were known as Smoothies.

Crombie overcoat

Button-down shirt

Shearling overcoat

Sweater vest

Cropped wool pants
More formal than jeans.

Mod-style dress/skirt

Heeled loafers

Sort—A female Suedehead

Soulies

Also known as Northern Soul, Soulie is a British dancing subculture that grew out of the Mod and Skinhead movements. The name derived from working-class youths' passion for American soul music, and was characterized by an expressive dancing style.

Northern England soul obsession

Soulies emerged in northern England as Mod was declining. Some developed an interest in American soul because of its new, funky sound and socially conscious lyrics; Soulies were particularly obsessed with finding obscure, fast-paced tracks, which they played at all-night dance clubs. The subculture emphasized individuality and self-expression as an escape from drab post-war reality. To release their emotions, Soulies would develop unique and acrobatic moves inspired by the music, including spins, high kicks and "backdrops."

Dress code

Bowling shirts or sleeveless pullovers with soul-club patches were paired with massive, high-waisted pants called "bags," and loafers or brogues. Female Soulies wore Mod-ish mini dresses or circle dresses and sandals.

CAUTION
TALCUM POWDER ON FLOOR

Some soul-music venues would dust their dance floors with talcum powder so dancers could perform slides and spins more easily.

Suspenders

Button-down shirt

Fair Isle sweater vest

Bowling shirt

"Bags"
Massive, high-waisted pants that kept dancers cool

Sharpies

The name "Sharpie" originated in Melbourne during the late 1960s and early 1970s, referring to a subculture of rebellious working-class youths who expressed themselves through vandalism and antisocial behavior, and were known for their sharp-looking fashion.

Aussie toughs

Sharpie subculture emerged in Australia during a period of rapid industrialization and urbanization, and the growth of working-class communities, providing a sense of identity and belonging for young people. Inspired by British Mod and Skinhead culture, Sharpies embraced distinct fashions and local rock music while asserting their working-class identity. The subculture was fueled by a desire to rebel against social exclusion through defiant fashion, crime and territory defense, highlighting the tensions faced by the younger generation.

Dress code

Sharpies were identifiable by their ultra-tight-fitting "Connie" cardigans, Harrington jackets, high-waisted pants, flannel shirts, skinny suspenders and boots. Their style was masculine, radical and intimidating, symbolic of their aggressive stance against authority.

❶ Straight-leg jeans
By the early 1970s, Sharpies had adopted regular straight-leg Levi's or Lee jeans.

❷ Treads
These open-toed basket-weave suede shoes had a top made of colored straps and a sole made from old car tires.

❸ High-waisted flared jeans
Flared, tight jeans by Australian brand Staggers were often worn by Sharpies at nightclubs.

Flat cap

Platform shoes

Skinny suspenders

4 Connie cardigan
This type of sweater, also known as a Conte cardigan, was tight-fitting, with a sharp striped pattern and a small buttoned "belt" at the back. The cardigans were often worn two sizes too small for an extra-tight fit.

5 Bluebird/little stars tattoos
The bluebird is a symbol of freedom, representing working-class Sharpies longing to break free from their class.

6 Gang T-shirt
These tees usually featured custom-made iron-on flocked letters.

7 Ban-Lon/Crestknit top
These knitwear tops were popular for both men and women.

8 Harrington jacket
This alternative to the Connie cardigan was also worn small, for a tight fit.

9 Lemon squeezers
These tight-fitting, high-waisted flared pants with pinstripes were often worn in nightclubs with a belt or suspenders.

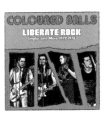

Coloured Balls
Emerging from the Sharpie subculture, Coloured Balls were known for their hard-rock sound and energetic performances. Their music spoke to Sharpies' working-class roots and rebellious spirit, and the band was a beloved symbol of the movement.

Hairstyles
For men, the signature "brush" cut had short, feathered hair on top and longer, mullet-like hair at the back.

The shuffle dance
The distinctive Sharpie dance derived from their confrontations with rival groups—e.g. Hippies. It involved a shuffling motion, and was sometimes done in groups, with an intimidating flailing of elbows and knees. The dance was often performed to hard-rock music.

Cholos

Cholo subculture originated in Southern California among Mexican and Chicano communities. It developed as a response to discrimination and marginalization, and drew heavily from indigenous and Mexican-American heritage.

Chicano pride

Cholo subculture emerged during the 1960s and 1970s, evolving from the Pachuco subculture of the 1940s. Cholos faced social and economic marginalization, and used their subculture to assert their identity and belonging. Street life played a significant role in shaping Cholo identity, with members often involved in activities like graffiti, breakdancing and forming neighborhood groups or gangs. Cholos embraced their indigenous roots and Mexican-American heritage, and developed their own slang, music, fashion and lifestyle.

Dress code

Cholos' bold, streetwise style is centered around comfort and group affiliation. It typically includes oversized clothing, monochrome color schemes, gold chains and bandannas.

❶ Pendleton shirt
Pendleton shirts are a symbol of pride in indigenous heritage. They are often worn over a white T-shirt and buttoned only at the top.

❷ Loose-fit chinos
Classic workwear in a straight or loose fit for comfort and mobility; Dickies and Ben Davis are popular choices.

Fedora

Dark sunglasses

Tank top

Bandanna

Dickies shorts

Knee-high white socks

Nike Cortez sneakers

Do-rag

Oversized white tee

Military web belt

Football/
baseball shirt

Gold jewelery

③ Rosary
These are worn by Catholics as a symbol of faith, spirituality and protection.

④ Creased jeans
To mimic zoot suit pants, Cholos sometimes iron their jeans to create a crease.

⑤ Tattoo
Tattoos are often large and highly visible. Common themes include religious iconography, gang-related symbols, Aztec or Mayan imagery and Gothic script.

⑥ Low riders
Low riders are cars modified with hydraulic systems that allow them to bounce and sway. They often have intricate custom paint jobs and airbrushed designs.

What is a Cholo?
Cholo is a Spanish word originally used to describe a mixed-race person of Native American and Spanish descent.

Chicano rapper Lil Rob

Chicano rap
This Hip-Hop subgenre of Mexican-American rappers blends traditional Mexican music with rap. It addresses street life, cultural pride and social issues.

Hairstyles
Cholos often sport shaved heads or slick, combed-back hair; some also wear hair nets.

Cholo slang
Cholos developed unique slang, including terms and phrases that are specific to their subculture.

Expression	Pronunciation	Meaning
Que onda	kay ohn-dah	"What's up?" Used to say hello.
Stay firme	stey feer-me	"Stay cool" or "stay strong." Used to say goodbye.
Simon	see-mohn	"Yes" or "for sure." Used to express agreement or affirm something.
La raza	la rah-sah	"The Race" or "The People," referring to the Mexican community.
Holmes	oh-meez	Derived from "homeboy," referring to a good friend or fellow gang member.
Vato	vah-toh	A guy or a dude, usually a friend or peer.
Ruca	roo-kah	A female friend, girlfriend or homegirl.

Dickies
The Texan brand started as a bib-overall company and evolved into a leader in workwear, gaining significant popularity in the streetwear scene.

Blossoming Revolution

Amid the tumult of the Vietnam War and the civil-rights movement, "flower power" emerged as a potent symbol of peace, unity and diversity. It intertwined fashion and sociopolitical advocacy, rejecting mainstream norms and championing inclusivity. Aligning style with civil-rights aspirations, the movement catalyzed societal shifts toward greater equity and diversity.

Flower Power (1965)

Vietnam War (1955–75)

"I have a dream" speech—Martin Luther King Jr. (1963)

Peacock Revolution

Hippies

The Hippie movement represented an alternative lifestyle centered around peace, love and freedom. It challenged societal norms, inspiring a generation to embrace open-mindedness and compassion.

Peace, love and psychedelics

The Hippie movement originated in the United States as a reaction to societal norms and political unrest, particularly the Vietnam War and the civil-rights movement. Predominantly consisting of white middle-class youth, this counterculture promoted peace, love and harmony, embracing a communal lifestyle and rejecting materialism. They were inspired by Eastern religions, psychedelic drugs and a desire to reconnect with nature. Key events like the Human Be-In and the Summer of Love solidified the movement's presence and popularity.

Maxi skirt

Dress code

Hippies drew inspiration from diverse cultures, embracing Indian paisley prints, Native American patterns and African motifs. They often used natural materials and made their own garments and accessories; this reflected the movement's values and spiritual influences.

1 Garland
Wearing wildflowers in one's hair was seen as a symbol of love and peace.

2 Mexican peasant blouse
Traditional Mexican cotton dresses and tops featured embroidery or lace trim and loose silhouettes. They were popular among Hippies for their comfortable, bohemian style and beautiful colors.

3 Headband
A headband could be made from a bandanna, a braided cord of leather, or beads.

Large, wide belt

Feather
headband

Water
buffalo sandals

④ Tie-dye T-shirt
Its handmade nature, psychedelic patterns and bright colors extol the Hippie ideology of embracing nature and altered states of mind.

⑤ Bell-bottom jeans
These flowing jeans were often decorated with patchwork, embroidery or paint.

⑥ Kaftan/dashiki
Associated with African and Middle Eastern cultures, these tops were embraced for their alternative, non-Western aesthetic.

⑦ Fringed vest
These were usually made of leather or suede with colorful embroidery or beads.

⑧ Statement accessories
Accessories often featured a peace symbol or flower motif. Wooden bangles and bracelets were also popular.

⑨ Peasant dress
These long dresses were made from layers of mismatched fabrics. The brightly colored patchwork elements contributed to the earthy, bohemian aesthetic.

Marijuana
Popular among Hippies for its ability to expand consciousness and connect with a greater sense of spirituality and creativity, pot was also believed to enhance sensory experiences and promote relaxation and peace.

Communal living
Communal living rejected the conventional nuclear family and capitalist system. It emphasized cooperation, egalitarianism and communal ownership, with shared resources and decentralized power. Many communes applied principles of sustainability, including organic farming, alternative energy and crafts.

Alternative religions
Hippies embraced a variety of Eastern philosophies that emphasized spirituality, consciousness and the nature of reality, which aligned with their values of non-violence, inner peace and the interconnectedness of all things.

Psychedelia
Psychedelic patterns were influenced by the use of drugs such as LSD. The vibrant colors and swirling shapes evoked the experience of drug use.

Folkies

The term "Folkies" derived from people—often young and well-educated—who share a passion for American and British folk music and its associations with political activism and social commentary.

Singing for social justice

American college enrollment doubled between the 1930s and the 1960s, ushering in a change in social attitude and raising awareness of world events and movements. Musicians including Bob Dylan and Joan Baez used folk music as a platform to express dissent and bring awareness to issues such as war, civil rights and social justice. This was consistent with traditional folk's storytelling roots; the music often served as a vehicle to express class issues through lyrics, making it easier to spread the message.

Dress code

Folkie clothing tended to be loose-fitting, a touch bohemian, and made from natural fibers such as cotton, linen, leather and wool. Both genders wore earth tones and embraced fringes, sandals and moccasins. Ethnic prints including paisley were also popular.

Bob Dylan

Dylan's early albums *The Freewheelin' Bob Dylan* and *The Times They Are a-Changin'* featured powerful political and social commentary, and shaped the sound and style of the folk movement.

Rustic hat

Shaggy hair

Paisley tie

Corduroy pants

Long, straight hair

Peasant blouse

Moccasins

Sandals

New Age Travelers

New Age Travelers espoused New Age beliefs and spent their time traveling between free music festivals; they were not traditionally nomadic, but chose to pursue the lifestyle and spiritual exploration.

Spiritual modern nomads

New Age Traveler culture evolved as a reaction to consumerism, materialism and societal upheaval. Adherents sought personal and spiritual growth by adopting a nomadic lifestyle that allowed them to reconnect with nature. Mostly made up of young English people influenced by the free festivals and hippie culture of the late 1960s, New Age Travelers often lived in vans or buses. They believed in mysticism, valued holistic wellness, and supported environmentalism.

Dress code

New Age Travelers drew influence from traditional Roma attire; they mixed and matched loose, baggy clothes—usually second-hand. Layers of bohemian-style clothing with ethnic-inspired patterns were accessorized with scarves and natural jewelry for cultural expression.

New Age spirituality
New Age spirituality focuses on personal growth and spiritual development. It draws on a wide range of religions and traditions, including Eastern practices, psychology and mythology.

Dreadlocks

Beard

Scarf

Fair Isle sweater

Patchwork elements
Clothing was often made from whatever resources they had, including scraps of fabric.

Layered ethnic jewelry

Ethnic-pattern robe

Black Panthers

This subculture was inspired by the political and social activism of the Black Panther Party. The group's name originated from the use of the black panther as a symbol of strength and resistance.

Black pride & power

Central to the Black Panther subculture were principles of racial equality, self-determination and community empowerment. Followers were encouraged to challenge systemic injustice and fight for their rights through various forms of activism, education and community service. Black Panthers championed a sense of pride in one's cultural heritage and emphasized the importance of unity and solidarity among marginalized groups.

Dress code

Black Panthers' clothing reflected the group's militant background. The color black was prominent as a symbol of power and resistance. Attire typically included black leather jackets, berets, dark sunglasses and military-style boots.

❶ Sunglasses
Sunglasses conveyed a sense of cool detachment while also protecting the eyes during confrontations with police.

❷ Military boots
These boots were a practical choice for the party's patrols and demonstrations, as well as a symbol of the party's militaristic stance.

Blue shirt

White turtleneck

Black skirt

Black pants

Medallion/
necklace

Black dress

Dashiki

③ Black leather jacket
This staple was often adorned
with the party's emblem or other
political symbols.

④ Mao's *Little Red Book*
The Black Panthers were influenced
by socialism, and saw it as a means to
achieve greater equality and justice.

⑤ Pinback buttons
Panthers often wore black-power pins
on their berets and jackets.

⑥ Black beret
Inspired by the French resistance's
green beret, it is a symbol of resistance
to police brutality.

Black Panther Party
Formed in 1966 by Huey P.
Newton and Bobby Seale in
Oakland, California, the party's
primary goal was to challenge
police brutality against
African-Americans through
community organizing, armed
self-defense, and the political
education and empowerment of
Black communities.

Armed patrol
To protect themselves against
police brutality and white
supremacist violence, the party
established armed patrols, a.k.a.
"copwatching," to monitor police
activity in Black neighborhoods
and intervene when they
witnessed abuse.

***Judas and the Black
Messiah* (2021)**
This film, based on a true story,
highlights the systemic racism
and oppression that African-
Americans faced in the 1960s,
and the government's attempts
to suppress the party's activism
and social movements.

Rudeboys

The name "rudeboy" comes from the Jamaican patois word *rude*, which means rough or tough. Rudeboys were often associated with violence and crime, but they were also known for their love of music and fashion.

Defiant Jamaican youth

Following Jamaica's independence from British rule in 1962, the country faced significant social and economic challenges, including widespread poverty and unemployment among the working class. Urban youths, in particular, felt marginalized and disenfranchised. As a result, Rudeboys emerged as an expression of defiance against these inequalities and as a means to assert their identity. Rudeboy attire and demeanor were influenced by sharp-dressed American gangsters and British Mods, symbolizing a sense of power and control in a society where they often felt powerless.

Dress code

Rudeboys embraced a sharp, sophisticated style with tailored suits, thin ties, porkpie hats, suspenders and polished shoes. Hairstyles were typically sleek and well-groomed, typically short with sharp side partings.

Porkpie hat/fedora

Sunglasses/ rounded eyewear

Skinny tie

Pocket square

Sharp tonic suit

Skinny or cuffed pants

Patent leather loafers

THE KING OF SKA

DEKKER

Musical influences

The music associated with Rudeboys has its roots in Jamaican ska and rocksteady, which eventually evolved into reggae. The rhythms and sounds of this music are known for reflecting the energy, passion and defiance of those who embraced it.

Rastas

The Rastafari movement, a.k.a. Rasta, is a spiritual, social and political movement that began in Jamaica. It seeks to empower and uplift people of African descent by advocating a return to their roots.

Christianity meets Afrocentrism

Rastafarianism emerged from a desire to resist the oppression and marginalization faced by Afro-Jamaicans during British colonial rule. As the movement gained momentum in the 1960s and 1970s, it created a unique culture and lifestyle centered around Pan-Africanism, self-reliance and a deep connection to nature. Ethiopia, considered the homeland for Rastafarians, symbolizes the aspiration for a unified Africa and the end of colonial domination. The global popularity of reggae music and artists like Bob Marley helped spread Rastafarian beliefs, values and aesthetics worldwide.

Dress code

Rastas' dress code is inspired by Ethiopian culture and the flag of the Ethiopian Royal Standard. It is characterized by natural, earthy colors and comfortable, loose-fitting garments. They typically wear traditional tunics, head wraps, and crocheted caps called "tams."

Rasta cap/"tam"

Long dreadlocks

Handmade jewelery

Loose-fit tunic

The origins of the name
The word "Rastafari" comes from *Ras Tafari*, the pre-coronation name of Haile Selassie I, the former Ethiopian emperor whom Rastas believe is the messiah. The lion on the flag is a symbol of the emperor.

Why dreadlocks?
Rastas' dreadlocks symbolize the "Lion of Judah," representing Emperor Haile Selassie and conveying strength, rejection of Western conformity, and divine connection to nature.

B-Boys

The term "B-Boy" comes from "break boy"—
a dancer who performs to the breakbeat in
Hip-Hop music. The subculture is a global dance
phenomenon that originated in the Bronx,
New York in the early 1970s.

Boogie down Bronx

B-Boy culture emerged as a
means of expression for young
African-American and Puerto
Rican youths in the Bronx, who
grappled with poverty, crime and
limited opportunities. B-Boy
battles started as a way for rival
gangs to settle disputes without
violence. Drawing inspiration
from a blend of martial arts,
gymnastics and African
and Latino dance styles, B-Boy
showdowns provided a creative
outlet and a positive alternative
amidst challenging surroundings.
The dance form gained worldwide
recognition in the 1980s and
1990s thanks to its exposure in
mainstream media and the ascent
of Hip-Hop culture.

Bucket hat

Gold chain

Wristband

Baggy
jeans

Low-top
sneakers

Dress code

The style emphasizes comfort
and functionality, and typically
includes loose-fitting clothing
that allows freedom of movement,
such as baggy pants, tracksuits
and sneakers. Dancers often
wear branded sportswear and
accessorize with hats, bandannas
or wristbands.

❶ T-shirt
Often plain, T-shirts might also
be decorated with graphics or logos.
Popular brands included Adidas,
Champion and Nike.

❷ Gloves
Gloves were often worn for
support, protection and to reduce
friction when dancing.

Cazal glasses

Flat cap

Windbreaker

Sports shorts

❸ Tracksuit
Loose-fitting nylon tracksuits allowed freedom of movement and facilitated floor sliding.

❹ Bandanna
Bandannas were often worn under hats, which was not only stylish but also helped with head spins.

❺ Boombox
Also known as a "ghetto blaster," a boombox was a portable stereo system that symbolized the urban style and street culture.

❻ Headband
These were worn to absorb sweat and keep dancers' hair out of their eyes.

❼ Baseball cap
Sometimes worn backwards, the caps were often printed with a crew logo or a brand.

❽ Athletic socks
Often in white or black with stripes or logos. Some wore knee-high socks.

Wild Style (1982)
This cult classic about a young graffiti artist in the South Bronx features performances by prominent B-Boys and graffiti artists.

Block parties
Street parties with MCs and DJs were the original venues for B-Boy performances and battles. They took place in residential areas and were usually hosted by locals who closed off the street to traffic, to make space for the event.

Uprock dancing
Uprock originated in the South Bronx, primarily among Puerto Ricans. Its fluid, rhythmic and acrobatic movements influenced breakdancing. It also introduced the concept of battles.

Adidas Superstar

Puma Clyde

Nike Air Force 1

Iconic B-Boy sneakers
Sneakers played an essential role in B-Boy subculture. They were not only fashionable but also functional for breakdancing.

Glam Rock

Glam emerged in the early 1970s as a fusion of rock 'n' roll with flamboyant fashion, make-up and performances. Its name reflects the visually striking and theatrical elements that define the subculture.

Androgyny rules
In response to the austerity of late 1960s Britain, a new genre of music emerged known as Glam Rock. The movement was inspired by theatrical pop stars like David Bowie, Marc Bolan and Elton John, and it celebrated spectacle, decadence and unapologetic artificiality. Songs were intended to shock with taboo references to androgyny, sexuality and life on Mars. The subculture was further shaped by the fascination with space exploration, futuristic themes and the emerging Disco scene, and incorporated these novel elements into its style.

Dress code
The fearless, over-the-top aesthetic defied traditional gender expectations. Male musicians often wore androgynous clothing such as silky blouses and feather boas paired with outrageous hairstyles and make-up.

❶ **Flashy matching set/jumpsuit**
Jumpsuits were often made from shiny or metallic fabric embellished with sequins, rhinestones and other glittery details.

❷ **Glittery jacket**
Shiny, reflective materials caught the light and sparkled on stage; silver, gold and red were popular colors.

Animal print

Silk scarf

❸ Velvet suit
Usually with wide lapels and flared pants, velvet suits were worn as a suit or as separates, often in bold colors or lavish patterns.

❹ Fringe/fur
Fringe and fur were often added to jackets, vests and other clothing, creating a sense of movement and drama when worn on stage.

❺ Bell-bottom pants
Often made from velvet, leather or corduroy, bell bottoms could be found in bright colors and wild prints.

❻ Statement accessories
Statement accessories such as oversized sunglasses, large rings, and other bold pieces were important components.

❼ Silky shirt
Billowy, loose-fitting shirts made of silk often had ruffled collars and cuffs. The silky fabric and androgynous cut represented the gender-bending spirit.

❽ Platform boots
Platforms had ultra-thick soles and high heels, and might be adorned with stars, flames or lightning bolts.

T. Rex, *Electric Warrior* (1971)
This album is widely regarded as one of the defining works of Glam Rock. With its combination of rock and pop hooks and sexualized lyrics, the album epitomized the hedonistic, boundary-pushing spirit.

Bowie stage jumpsuit designed by Kansai Yamamoto.

Ziggy Stardust (1972)
David Bowie is widely considered the icon of Glam Rock. He created the fictional rock-star persona Ziggy Stardust, a flamboyant and androgynous alien with an otherworldly appearance, accompanied by Bowie's sci-fi-themed music.

Hair & make-up
Make-up was usually bold and theatrical, featuring striking eye shadow, glitter and dramatic eyeliner. Hairstyles were often wildly teased and might involve vibrant colors, adding to the larger-than-life persona.

Mr. Freedom
This iconic London boutique epitomized Glam Rock style. Owned by designer Tommy Roberts, it featured fashion by young commissioned designers.

Disco

The name Disco was derived from *discothèque*, the French term for a nightclub with recorded music. This vibrant subculture became synonymous with dancing, fashion and nightlife.

Cultural fusion on the dance floor

Disco emerged in the early 1970s as a reaction to the social and political climate, providing a haven for marginalized groups such as African-Americans, Latinos and sexual minorities. Originating in underground clubs in New York, its danceable beats and repetitive hooks soon gained mainstream popularity, resulting in iconic hits like the Bee Gees' "Stayin' Alive." Disco was a melting pot of cultures, with various ethnic, musical and artistic influences resulting in vibrant and eclectic clothing styles.

Dress code

Extravagant and glamorous, Disco fashion featured bright colors and shimmering fabrics. Typical attire included bell-bottom pants, wide-collar shirts, flowy dresses and jumpsuits.

❶ **Halston dress**

Halston was the most iconic designer of the era. His designs featured graceful, feminine silhouettes including sexy halter-necks and off-shoulder designs. His lightweight, silky and metallic fabrics were comfortable and beautiful to wear, and allowed movement on the dance floor.

Faux-fur coat

Wide-collar shirt

Flared pants

Platform shoes

2 Metallic cropped top
Made from shiny, reflective fabrics like lamé or Lurex, cropped tops exposed the midriff and often featured design details including fringe or a cowl neck.

3 Flowy wrap dress
Designer Diane von Furstenberg made her name in the 1970s with her signature wrap dress. The flattering, feminine style was made from lightweight fabrics such as jersey, and featured bold prints and colors.

4 Oversized sunglasses
The bold, statement-making style allowed Disco dancers to shield their eyes from the bright lights of the dance floor.

5 Leisure suit
The two-piece leisure suit featured a shirt-like jacket with wide lapels, matching pants, and often a brightly colored shirt worn underneath.

6 Elegant jumpsuit
One-piece jumpsuits were a practical and stylish choice, with a soft drape that would swing with dance moves. Often in bold patterns or colors, some were embellished with sequins or made from glittery fabric.

Chunky jewelry

Cropped top with bell sleeves

Platform shoes

Studio 54
New York disco Studio 54 was famous for its celebrity guests and hedonistic, exclusive parties. Frequent guests, including Andy Warhol, Bianca Jagger and Liza Minnelli, made it an iconic symbol of the era's excess and glamour.

***Saturday Night Fever* (1977)**
This blockbuster movie explored themes of class, race and gender in the context of the subculture.

Grace Jones
Grace Jones was a model, singer and performer; her music and fashion helped define the era's experimental style. She became famous for her edgy, androgynous look, pushing the boundaries of gender norms and fashion conventions.

New Romantics

The New Romantic movement emerged in the late 1970s as an escape from the bleakness and nihilism of Punk. It celebrated glamour, fashion and individuality, and had a strong connection to music and art.

Kings of the synth frontier

Focused on glamour, fashion and a sense of theatricality, the New Romantics embraced an optimistic and idealistic attitude. The movement started in London's club scene, where creatives found inspiration in the rich visuals and symbolism of past eras, incorporating them into their eclectic style. Heavily influenced by Glam Rock, art and literature, key bands included Visage, Duran Duran and Spandau Ballet, who combined synth-pop sounds with elaborate stage performances and a strong focus on visual aesthetics.

Dress code

Flamboyant, often androgynous outfits were inspired by historical fashions (such as Victorian and Rococo) as well as sci-fi and theatrical costumes. Key elements included frilled shirts, velvet jackets and extravagant accessories, often paired with dramatic hair and make-up.

Vintage costumes

High-shine fabric

Winklepickers

Pleated
pegged pants

Frilly tie/
Victorian cravat

❶ Frock coat
Long wool coats inspired by
Regency-era fashions, popular in
Britain in the early 1800s, gave a sense
of swashbuckling romanticism and
dandyish flair.

❷ Synthesizer
Synthesizers allowed musicians
to create sounds that were not possible
with traditional instruments. They
were also used to create futuristic
electronic soundscapes.

❸ Military jacket
Vintage military jackets—or modern
interpretations—were influenced
by Weimar Berlin, France's *Incroyables*
and British royalty. The jackets were
often made from velvet and decorated
with braids, studs or gold buttons.

❹ Elaborate headdress
Historical-inspired headdresses, such
as pirate-style tricorns, turbans and
bowler hats, were adorned with lavish
embellishments including brooches,
rhinestones and feathers.

❺ Poet shirt
The billowy, long-sleeved poet shirt,
inspired by the Romantic era, was
often accented with ruffles, ribbon ties
or gathered necklines and cuffs.

Blitz kids
Blitz, a club in London's Covent
Garden, provided a platform for New
Romantic bands and their fans to
showcase their creativity and fashion
sense. Located between two art
colleges (St. Martin's and the Central
School of Art), it became a hotbed
for fashion students who set London
ablaze during the 1980s.

Visage, *Fade to Grey* (1980)

Alternative to Punk
New Romantic music showcased
a blend of synthesizers, electronic
beats and poetic lyrics, creating a
distinctive sound that celebrated
glamour and artistic expression, and
became a major influence on the
development of the synth-pop and
electronica genres.

Vivienne
Westwood's
Pirate
collection
(1981)

Key designer
Vivienne
Westwood
began her
romantic ideas
with adaptations
of dandified
Regency
designs; later,
she developed
them into
a pirate look.

The Neon

The Neon Era, synonymous with the 1980s, was characterized by vibrant, over-the-top fashion mirroring the decade's materialism and burgeoning economic confidence. This period, marked by the mantra "greed is good," saw an explosion of individualistic expressions in fashion and subcultures, encapsulating the era's cultural shifts and economic exuberance.

Economic Recovery Tax Act (1981)

Era

Back to the Future (1985)

IBM Personal Computer (1981)

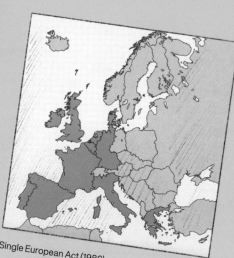

Single European Act (1986)

MTV Channel (1981)

Neo-Baroque

The dramatic Neo-Baroque style emerged in the 1980s, drawing inspiration from the opulence and extravagance of the Baroque period, which was characterized by bold colors, ornate patterns and luxurious fabrics.

Dress for excess

The return to extravagance in fashion was driven by a desire for self-expression and luxury following a period of minimalist trends. High-profile designers including Christian Lacroix, Thierry Mugler and Jean Paul Gaultier incorporated dramatic historical references, bold colors and over-the-top accessories into their designs, creating collections that were glamorous and decadent. The trend became popular in the 1980s, a time of excess and extravagance when people wanted to show off their wealth and status.

Dress code

Rich fabrics like velvet, brocade and taffeta were often intricately embroidered with ornate patterns. Silhouettes emphasized volume and drama; fitted waists, puff sleeves, and voluminous skirts were styled with lavish, flamboyant jewelry.

Theatrical outerwear

Christian Lacroix, AW89

Baroque-inspired prints

Gianni Versace, SS92

❶ Ball gown
Full-length gowns reflected the era's love of excess and glamour. Voluminous skirts were made of rich fabrics with extravagant details including puff sleeves and heavy embellishments.

❷ Brocade jacket
Luxurious, ornate garments featured elaborate patterns and textures, and were typically made of rich materials including silk, velvet and metallic threads.

❸ Puffball dress
The voluminous, short cocktail dress had a large billowed skirt and a tight bodice. One of its most iconic representations was the Pouf dress by Christian Lacroix.

❹ Corseted design
This modern interpretation of decadent fashion from the Baroque era featured lace or embroidery and boning, creating a dramatic, silhouette-enhancing effect.

❺ Opulent jewelry
Extravagant necklaces, oversized earrings, brooches and bracelets featured intricate designs.

❻ Ornate heels
Made from rich materials and embellished with bows, buckles and beads, heels were sometimes also embroidered with metallic threads.

Puff sleeves

Silk scarf

An era of extravagance
The Baroque period was an artistic movement that originated in Italy during the late 16th century. It was characterized by dramatic, exuberant and extravagant styles in fashion and architecture.

Iconic design
Jean Paul Gaultier designed the stagewear for Madonna's 1990 *Blond Ambition* tour, including her Cone Bra bodysuit.

Madonna, *Like a Virgin* (1984)

Material world
Economic prosperity, corporate deregulation and media promotion fueled materialism in the 1980s. The Reagan era's "greed is good" ethos and emphasis on status symbols influenced culture. Neo-Baroque style's over-the-top decorative qualities resonated with the flashy culture.

Power Dressing

Born out of the need for women to be taken seriously in the workplace, Power Dressing was characterized by clothing that exuded confidence, authority and professionalism. It was a symbol of empowerment, strength and success.

A suit to command the boardroom

The socioeconomic landscape shifted in the 1980s as women increasingly joined the workforce and sought equal opportunities in male-dominated spaces.
To assert power and competence in workplaces where wearing traditional feminine attire risked undermining their authority, many women in the 1980s adopted menswear-inspired suits. The style was epitomized by large shoulder pads, tailored suits and bold accessories. Popularized by mass media and characters on *Dynasty*, the style signified professionalism, authority and ambition for career women seeking to establish themselves in corporate culture.

Dress code

Power Dressing emphasized clean lines, structured tailoring and assertive silhouettes. Men's suiting fabrics were common, and colors leaned toward neutral and dark tones for a professional, commanding appearance. Bold statement accessories exuded confidence and authority.

➊ Power suit
The epitome of Power Dressing, the power suit features tailored jackets and matching pants or a pencil skirt, often made from traditional men's suiting materials.

Polka dots

Pussy-bow blouse

Pencil skirt

Pantyhose

Pointy pumps

Shoulder-padded dress

Oversized outerwear

Shoulder-padded jacket

---

② Power blouse
Voluminous sleeves and/or shoulder pads create the illusion of broad shoulders. The blouses were made from silky fabric and often tied at the neck.

③ Wide belt
Often made of leather and worn over a coat, blazer or dress, a wide belt helps define the waist.

④ Stiletto pumps
Pointed toes and high heels create a taller, stronger look for women.

⑤ Statement jewelry
Bold, eye-catching jewelry, such as large earrings, necklaces or brooches, add visual impact and signify power and wealth.

⑥ High-waisted pants
The style projects strength and confidence; the pants often had pleats and a wide-leg silhouette.

⑦ Structured handbag
Handbags came in boxy shapes—either with a handle or without (a clutch).

Dynasty (1981–89)
The TV series featured powerful women in glamorous outfits. Joan Collins and Linda Evans played two women battling for control of an oil empire. Their wardrobes defined the power look of the era and inspired many real-world women in business.

Giorgio Armani suit
Armani's iconic power suit was characterized by its clean lines, impeccable tailoring and luxurious materials. The suit still symbolizes success and power.

Keep it short
Short hairstyles conveyed masculinity, authority and practicality—a woman with a busy professional lifestyle. The cut projected a competent, no-nonsense image, showcased statement earrings and avoided the issue of long locks clashing with large shoulder pads.

Aerobics

Aerobics style, synonymous with the fitness craze of the 1980s, is a vibrant and energetic look that reflects the spirit of the dance-based cardiovascular workout.

Let's get physical

Aerobics transformed from a niche fitness routine into a mainstream phenomenon in the 1980s. Celebrities including Jane Fonda and Richard Simmons played a significant role in popularizing the trend with their workout videos and TV shows. The style represented a new, fun and fashionable approach to fitness, departing from the male-dominant gym scene and encouraging individuals, especially women, to take up exercise. Marketers promoted the "healthy is beautiful" image, and the lively Disco-inspired fashions associated with aerobics spread into leisure and club wear.

Dress code

Aerobics gear was characterized by neon colors, bold patterns and shiny, stretchy fabrics. Classic elements include high-cut leotards, leggings and leg warmers worn with headbands or sweatbands and athletic sneakers.

❶ Headband/sweatband
These were worn on wrists and around the head to absorb sweat and keep hair tucked away.

❷ Unitard
These skintight, one-piece garments were often layered with leotards or cropped tops.

❸ Sports shorts
Lightweight nylon shorts were worn by men; women often layered them with tights.

Tank top

Sneakers

Ballet slippers

Color-block windbreaker

Colored hand weights

Bike shorts

Cropped top

❹ Leg warmers
These knitted accessories were worn over leggings or tights for an extra pop of color as well as to keep muscles warm.

❺ Reebok Freestyle sneakers
The Freestyle was a high-top design with padded ankles and soft soles that provided support and cushioning.

❻ Neon tights
Bold, vibrant tights in neon colors like pink, green and orange were often worn under shorts or leotards.

❼ French-cut leotard with belt
"French-cut" means cut high on the thigh. Belts were worn on top to help define the waistline.

❽ Off-the-shoulder T-shirt/sweatshirt
Made popular by the movie *Flashdance*, slouchy, oversized T-shirts and sweatshirts were worn off one shoulder to show a hint of skin.

Upbeat pop tracks
Aerobic music was upbeat and energetic, featuring pop and Disco hits including "Physical" and "I'm So Excited." Their fast tempo and catchy beats made them ideal for aerobic dance routines.

Jane Fonda's Workout Book
Published in 1981, Fonda's book provided a comprehensive guide to aerobic exercise, including step-by-step instructions and photographs as well as nutritional advice and lifestyle tips.

Reebok Freestyle advertisement

Branded sportswear
Brands like Reebok, Nike and Danskin produced workout clothes designed for aerobics. Logos and brand names established a sense of community and identity among enthusiasts.

Voguers

Voguer subculture first emerged in the 1970s, in the gay Black and Latino communities of Harlem. The name alludes to "voguing," a style of dance inspired by the glamorous poses of models in *Vogue* magazine.

A safe haven for minorities
Voguing began as a way for marginalized people to express themselves and find acceptance, empowerment and self-confidence. In the 1960s, sexual minorities, as well as people of color, suffered from discrimination and violent assaults. As a reaction to this, drag balls, influenced by the Harlem ballroom scene and the underground club circuit, became an exclusive safe space. Ball participants would compete in order to showcase their creativity, dancing skills and fashion style.

Dress code
Voguers dress up to make a statement and stand out. Their bold, extravagant style is usually inspired by the world of high fashion. Participants often wear custom-made outfits in vibrant colors and luxurious fabrics with eye-catching accessories.

Glitter make-up

Large earrings

Gloves

Bodysuit
Provides comfort and freedom of movement.

Metallic or sequined elements

Paris Is Burning (1990)

Club Kids

The Club Kid subculture emerged as part of New York City's vibrant nightlife scene. Club Kids were known for their outrageous attire, wild antics and—as the name implies—love of clubbing.

Celebration & self-expression

Made up of predominantly sexual minorities and gender-fluid young New Yorkers, Club Kids preached hedonism, flamboyance and creative self-expression. Nightclubs were the only places where they felt free to dress in outlandish costumes and celebrate their identity and sexuality. Inspired by Andy Warhol's Factory and its inhabitants, the Club Kids saw themselves as living works of art, embracing avant-garde fashion and attention-grabbing performances, and hosting extravagant, often illegal, parties.

Dress code

Club Kids' theatrical style was childish and playful. Outrageously flamboyant costumes in vibrant colors and unconventional materials displayed a sense of individualism and artistry. Childish items such as school bags and lunch boxes were common accessories.

Over-the-top hairstyle

Neon-colored hair/wig

Face piercings

Theatrical make-up/ face paint

Androgynous clothing

Fishnet stockings

Custom platform shoes

Astro Erle
A prominent figure in the 1990s New York club scene, Erle was known for his towering 24-inch platform shoes.

Bosozoku

Bosozoku (暴走族) is a flashy gang known for riding noisy customized motorcycles. The name means "violent running tribe," reflecting their rebellious reputation and disregard for societal norms.

Speed, danger & defiance

Bosozoku subculture emerged in the 1970s among Japanese youth, inspired by the rebellious spirit of American biker gangs and the growing popularity of motorcycles. Preceding Bosozoku, 1950s *Kaminari Zoku* ("thunder tribe"), formed by ex-Kamikaze pilots, laid the foundation for this nonconformist subculture. Economic pressures and social unrest contributed to the rise of Bosozoku; members often engaged in illegal street racing and violent clashes with rival gangs or law enforcement. They rebelled against conformist society, finding excitement in speed, danger and defying authority.

Dress code

Bosozoku embraced a mix of rebellious and military-inspired styles, often with oversized clothing featuring bold kanji slogans and gang symbols. The attire commonly included military-style boots, leather or military jackets, and traditional Japanese clothing and accessories.

❶ Mask
Long surgical masks are worn to cover the face, offering anonymity and a unique, intimidating appearance as well as protection during high-speed rides.

❷ Tasuki sash
This traditional item is used to hold kimonos in place for mobility.

Haramaki

Boiler suit

Baggy pants

Sunglasses

Gloves

Jika-tabi

Half helmet
(Marushin W116)

③ Tokko-fuku
Translated as "special attack clothing," a tokko-fuku is an elaborately embroidered suit or jumpsuit inspired by workwear and WWII kamikaze pilots' suits. They are adorned with personalized slogans, gang logos, kanji and imperial Japan flags.

④ Black leather jacket
This biker staple was adopted by Bosozoku members in the 1970s.

⑤ Military boots
Drawing influence from military attire, these boots convey a sense of power and toughness.

⑥ Hachimaki
This traditional item was worn by samurais to strengthen the spirit and keep the wearer safe from evil spirits and demons.

⑦ Weapons
Bosozoku use a baseball bat or bokken, a traditional wooden sword used for training.

Honda CB/CM series
These motorcycles were popular for their big engines and affordability. They were often customized with a loud exhaust system, oversized fairings, and tucked-in handlebars. Fenders and gas tanks were often painted with motifs such as flames or the Rising Sun flag.

Extreme pompadours
Gravity-defying hairstyles served as a show of rebellion and a way to stand out from the crowd.

Imperial Japanese symbols
Bosozoku use the Rising Sun flag and Imperial Seal as a rejection of modern, Westernized Japan. They symbolize national pride and a nostalgic view of the country's past.

Sukeban

Sukeban subculture is centered around delinquent high-school girls. The term (スケバン) comes from the Japanese words *suke* (female) and *ban* (boss), signifying a girl gang leader.

Schoolgirl gangs

Sukeban originated as a response to the strict societal expectations placed on Japanese girls. These young women chose to defy traditional gender roles and express their rebelliousness through fashion and behavior. Sukeban groups formed in schools, providing a sense of camaraderie and empowerment. They gained notoriety for their acts of defiance, such as smoking, fighting and participating in other delinquent activities, which garnered media attention and further popularized the subculture.

Dress code

The look is characterized by long skirts and sailor-style school uniforms. Accessories such as surgical masks were often worn to conceal their identity. They wear bold make-up and dye their hair unnatural colors.

Sukeban Deka (1975–82)
A manga classic. The TV series followed Saki Asamiya, a high-school student who is recruited by the police to go undercover as a delinquent and solve crimes.

Brightly colored/permed hair

Weapon: *shinai*

Sailor uniform

Cropped top

Rolled-up sleeves

Long, pleated skirt
Traditional Japanese school uniforms typically feature above-the-knee skirts. By wearing long skirts, Sukeban girls express their nonconformity.

Feminist slogan in kanji

Otaku

Otaku is a term used to describe people with obsessive interests, particularly anime and manga. The word originates from a casual second-person pronoun, お宅, which means "your house" in Japanese.

Fandom-fueled style

In the 1980s, Japan's economic boom and the rise of home entertainment created a golden age of anime, with popular shows like *Gundam* and *Dragon Ball* captivating young audiences. *Otaku,* or those with excessive enthusiasm for anime and manga, emerged as a subculture and formed communities around their hobbies. Despite its origins, the term has been used to refer to a variety of obsessive, nerdy subcultures. While the name still has a negative connotation, Otaku has evolved into a global phenomenon.

Dress code

Otaku have a distinctive geeky look, often wearing neat shirts and pants and nerdy glasses paired with long, stringy hair or buzz cuts. Some wear clothing and accessories inspired by anime, manga and video-game characters.

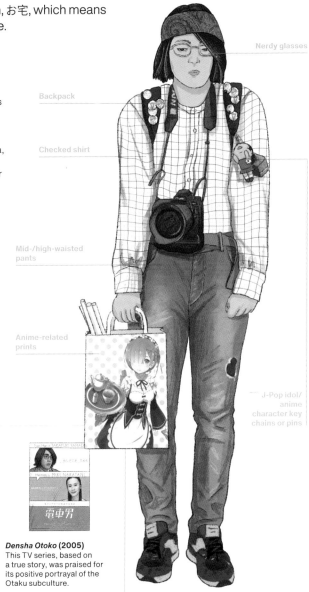

Nerdy glasses

Backpack

Checked shirt

Mid-/high-waisted pants

Anime-related prints

J-Pop idol/ anime character key chains or pins

Cosplay culture

Otaku cosplay to express love for characters and series, showcase creativity and connect with like-minded fans. Cosplay immerses them in the anime/manga world, fueling their passion.

Densha Otoko (2005)
This TV series, based on a true story, was praised for its positive portrayal of the Otaku subculture.

Bogans

Known for their working-class pride and strong sense of identity, Bogans have carved out a distinct place in their societies, challenging mainstream norms and embracing their heritage.

Flannies, flip-flops & AC/DC

Bogan subculture arose during the 1970s and 1980s in Australia and New Zealand as a response to the decline of manufacturing industries and the rise of urbanization and globalization. Bogans embraced their working-class roots and developed a strong patriotic identity, celebrating their connection to the land and their communities. Their style and preferences highlight this pride, often incorporating symbols of national heritage and local traditions while resisting mainstream consumerism and global influences.

Dress code

Characterized by a casual and laid-back style, Bogan clothing is comfortable and practical. The look typically includes jeans, work boots, and tees featuring band logos or other symbols of the subculture. Trucker hats and mullets complete the aesthetic.

❶ Tank top
This sleeveless tee is a Bogan staple. Although it comes in many colors, navy blue is the classic choice, especially among shearers.

❷ Flannel shirt
A flannel shirt is called a "flannie" in Australian slang. It is usually worn as a jacket over a tank top, or tied around the waist.

❸ Ugg boots
These sheepskin boots, originally from Australia, were popular among shearers due to their resistance to lanolin. They were also worn for warmth and comfort at home.

Sunglasses

Trucker hat

Sleeveless flannie

Bandanna

Beanie

Work boots

Sweatpants

Cuts/cut-offs

❹ Aussie thongs
Rubber-soled flip-flops are a classic Australian item. They are sometimes worn with socks.

❺ Stubbies shorts
Stubbies is an Australian brand, and the shorts are designed as workwear.

❻ Band T-shirt
Black T-shirts feature logos or artwork of favorite Aussie rock bands such as AC/DC or Midnight Oil.

❼ VB beer
Victoria Bitter (VB) beer is widely available throughout Australia and is often associated with blue-collar workers, particularly in the state of Victoria, where it's the best-selling beer.

Offensive or a source of pride?
The term "Bogan" was voted one of Australia's most objectionable words because it is thought by some to stereotype people of lower socioeconomic status. However, some argue that it gives marginalized groups a voice and a source of pride.

Southern Cross
Bogans often had this symbol of Australian pride tattooed on their arms.

Australian-made cars
Assembled in Australia, the Holden Commodore was an affordable, powerful sedan that represented a masculine, rebellious spirit. It became a symbol of Bogan pride and all things loudly Australian.

The Mullet
Mullet hairstyles—short at the front and sides, long at the back—are popular for both men and women; mustaches are often spotted on men.

Preppies

Preppy style is a timeless classic characterized by a polished casual appearance often associated with wealth and privilege. Derived from "preparatory," the term referred to students attending elite college-prep schools in the northeastern United States.

The smart set

Preppy style emerged in the late 1970s as affluent youth embraced the conservative looks of their prep-school uniforms. They embraced the style to differentiate themselves from anti-establishment trends, and challenged the traditional attire by incorporating elements heavily influenced by sportswear, reflecting their participation in upscale sports like sailing and tennis. From the Ivy League style of the 1950s to the Preppy style, American collegiate looks pushed the boundaries and traditions of elite society while maintaining social-status symbolism.

Dress code

The Preppy look was characterized by classic, conservative clothing in bold colors, plaids and stripes. Key items included button-down Oxford shirts, polo shirts, khaki pants and cable-knit sweaters in uplifting shades of pink, blue, green and yellow.

❶ **Club blazer**
This staple, popular for both men and women, featured brass buttons that were often embossed with a nautical or collegiate motif.

❷ **Button-down Oxford shirt**
The American classic collegiate staple was typically worn in pastels, neutral colors or Bengal stripes.

School tie

Pearl necklace

Cable-knit sweater

A-line plaid skirt

Penny loafers

Cricket sweater

Tweed sport coat

Canvas/
braided belt

Rugby shirt

Boat shoes

Tennis skirt

❸ Nantucket red pants
Named after the vacation destination in Massachusetts, these chino-style pants were made from faded red cotton canvas.

❹ Polo shirt
Originally athletic wear, polo shirts became popular in bright colors by brands including Lacoste and Polo Ralph Lauren.

❺ Madras fabric
This light, summery cotton fabric featured a distinctive plaid pattern in bright colors. It was named after the Indian city of Madras (now Chennai), where it originated.

The Official Preppy Handbook (1980)
This satirical book by Lisa Birnbach poked fun at Preppy culture, fashions and lifestyle. The book was an instant bestseller and remains a cultural touchstone.

Polo Ralph Lauren
Ralph Lauren was synonymous with Preppy style. His Polo brand featured classic silhouettes, equestrian and nautical motifs and traditional fabrics. His designs embodied elite Americana and popularized the Preppy lifestyle.

Put your name on it
Monogramming is seen as a way to display one's social status and wealth. A monogram features a person's initials or the initials of a family member or significant other.

Sloane Rangers

The term "Sloane Ranger" emerged in the late 1970s to describe a particular type of upper-middle-class British youth. The name originates from Sloane Square in Chelsea, London, an area known for its affluent residents.

Posh traditionalists

Sloane Ranger subculture surfaced as a counterpoint to growing countercultural movements. Sloanes, cherishing their privileged origins, attended elite schools and embraced a traditional British—and undeniably posh—way of life. Their love for countryside activities such as horseback riding and hunting heavily influenced their look, blending urban sophistication with rural practicality. *The Official Sloane Ranger Handbook*, a satirical guide published in 1982, popularized the term and codified the subculture's behaviors, habits and aesthetic inclinations.

Dress code

Sloanes championed a conservative, preppy aesthetic, marrying city elegance with country durability. Perennially classic and understated, the style featured quality fabrics and timeless cuts. Men typically wore tailored suits, while women favored twinsets, pearls and tweed skirts.

❶ Highland cashmere sweater
This Scottish classic is a luxurious staple. Its quality and heritage align with Sloanes' appreciation for comfort and understated elegance.

❷ Pleated skirt
Often knee or calf length, pleated skirts reflect conservatism and modesty.

Button-down shirt

Hacking jacket

Loafers

Kitten heels

Pearl jewelry

Twin sets

Wool flat cap

Corduroy pants

③ Piecrust-collar blouse
The Edwardian-inspired high, ruffled neckline is a nod to the romantic and conservative style.

④ Tweed skirt
Tweed, with its Scottish origins and association with country sports, was often worn as pencil or A-line skirts.

⑤ Hunter Wellington boots
These waterproof rubber boots are essential for country living. The classic design and durable construction make them perfect for muddy British weather.

⑥ Trench coat
Its military origins, functionality and association with British brand Burberry make it an ideal piece for the unpredictable British weather and Sloane style.

⑦ Chelsea boots
Originating in the Victorian era—and named after the fashionable Chelsea area—these ankle boots are known for their elastic side panels and pull tabs at the back.

⑧ Hermès scarf
A symbol of luxury and sophistication, the *carré's* intricate design and high-quality silk material represented Sloanes' appreciation for fine craftsmanship and classic style.

⑨ Barbour waxed jacket
Originating in the early 20th century, this iconic outerwear is known for its durable waxed cotton, corduroy collar and tartan lining.

The Official Sloane Ranger Handbook (1982)
The humorous yet insightful guide detailed the lifestyle, mannerisms and fashion of the subculture and made "Sloane Ranger" a staple term in British sociolinguistics.

Princess Diana
Known for her classic, elegant style, Princess Diana was often referred to as the Sloane Rangers' leader.

PURDEY
Gun & Rifle Makers
LONDON 1814

Traditional British brands
The timeless aesthetics, quality craftsmanship and heritage appeal of traditional British brands such as Purdey and Hunter aligned with the subculture's pursuit of understated elegance and functionality, and also reflected Sloanes' love for country pursuits.

Story

The Sound of Rebellion

Rock music has always been a forum for dissent. From its early roots in the 1950s to its many offshoots today, it has been the soundtrack of countercultural movements and the voice of the disenchanted, and each subgenre reflects a unique aspect of defiance.

Chuck Berry

Siouxsie and the Banshees

Elvis Presley

Judas Priest

❶ Rock 'n' roll
Early rock 'n' roll rhapsodized about teenage angst and personal freedom; lyrics often dealt with heartbreak, dancing and fast cars.
♬
Upbeat, danceable rhythms, simple chord progressions, and a focus on electric guitars and drums.

❷ Goth
Goth is known for its melancholic and introspective lyrics, as well as existentialism, sorrow and romanticism.
♬
Atmospheric and echoey guitars, synthesizers, deep bass lines and haunting vocals.

❸ Metal
With its power and aggression, metal explores topics such as war, violence and the darker aspects of human nature.
♬
Heavily distorted guitars, fast guitar solos, aggressive drumming and powerful vocals.

Nine Inch Nails

Nirvana

The Clash

Pearl Jam

Pearl Jam

❹ Industrial

Industrial music explores dystopian themes including societal control, oppression and technological alienation.

♫

Repetitive, machinelike beats, distorted vocals and non-traditional instrumentation including synthesizers and machinery sounds.

❺ Punk

Political and confrontational, Punk challenged societal norms and expressed a sense of anger and dissatisfaction.

♫

A raw sound, fast tempos and short songs. The music often featured simple three-chord structures and abrasive vocals.

❻ Grunge

Angst-filled Grunge often addresses themes such as social alienation, apathy, confinement and a desire for freedom.

♫

Heavy, distorted guitar sounds, slow, brooding tempos. Grunge often features a sense of rawness and authenticity.

Metalheads

Metalhead subculture derived its name from heavy metal music. The term emerged in the 1970s to describe fans who were as hard, heavy and nonconformist as the music they adored.

Raging against norms

Metalhead subculture originated in the 1970s, a period marked by the Vietnam War, social upheaval and economic instability. Bands like Black Sabbath, Led Zeppelin and Judas Priest gave birth to the heavy metal genre, offering a raw and powerful sonic response to tumultuous times. Metalheads resonated with the defiant spirit of the music, using it as a cathartic outlet for their anxieties and as a form of rebellion against the conservatism of mainstream society.

Dress code

Metalhead attire is predominantly dark and edgy, with an unrefined, rugged look that rejects mainstream trends. The look often includes black leather, denim, militia elements and metal studs, and accessories feature skulls, crosses and other Gothic motifs.

❶ Leather jacket
Often black, leather jackets may be adorned with patches, studs and band logos. They are popular due to their tough, rebellious appearance, which is reminiscent of biker subculture.

❷ Denim vest
These vests—also known as "battle vests"—became popular in the '80s and are still a favorite. They're often worn over band T-shirts, and are decorated with patches or band logos.

❸ Band patches
Sewn onto jackets or vests, these patches represent a Metalhead's concert history, and their musical tastes and affiliations.

Long hair

Boots with metal studs

Leather pants

Denim jacket

Bandanna

High-top sneakers

4 Band T-shirt
These staples of the Metalhead wardrobe feature the logos or album art of favorite bands.

5 Skull jewelry
Skulls are a common motif in metal culture, symbolizing themes of mortality that are often explored in the music.

6 Spiked or studded accessories
Wristbands, belts or collars with spikes or studs are often worn. They add to the aggressive, rebellious aesthetic that is a hallmark of Metalhead subculture.

7 Black jeans
Often ripped or distressed, black jeans are popular due to their versatile and edgy look.

8 Bullet belt
Originating in the Punk scene, belts made from bullet casings are often associated with thrash metal and symbolize an anti-establishment attitude.

9 Combat boots
These boots symbolize the gritty, aggressive nature of metal music. Originally military footwear, their adoption by the Punk and metal scenes has made them a subculture staple.

Devil horns
Also known as "metal horns," the gesture was made famous by Ronnie James Dio. Originally borrowed from his Italian grandmother to ward off the evil eye, the sign now primarily represents unity and a shared love of heavy metal music.

Wacken Open Air
This German heavy metal festival is a mecca for Metalheads. The annual event attracts fans from all over the world with its lineup of bands from diverse metal subgenres.

Judas Priest, *Hell Bent for Leather* (1978)

Headbanging
Headbanging is a signature move of Metalheads. Shaking their heads vigorously up and down with the music is a physical expression of enthusiasm and appreciation.

Punks

The term "punk" comes from 1960s slang meaning worthless. The rebellious youth subculture symbolized a raw, anarchic response to mainstream societal norms, expressed through aggressive music, in-your-face fashions and a defiant attitude.

The sound of anarchy

Punk originated in the 1970s as a countercultural movement—a reaction to the perceived excesses of mainstream 1970s society and music. Its roots were intertwined with economic strife and the disillusionment of the era's young people. Punk music, characterized by its aggressive, hard-edged sound, short songs and political or anti-establishment lyrics, catalyzed the movement. Bands like the Sex Pistols and the Ramones were pivotal; their provocative performances and anti-establishment messages resonated with a disaffected generation.

Dress code

Punk fashion flaunts aggressive nonconformity. It involves an unconventional mix of military gear, band T-shirts and DIY to create a distinctive and shocking look. Key patterns and materials include tartan, leather and metal studs.

❶ DIY leather jacket
A quintessential Punk staple, the leather jacket—usually black—was typically adorned with patches, studs or painted designs.

❷ Patches & pins
Often featured band logos, political messages or symbols associated with the subculture.

❸ Tartan
The Royal Stewart tartan was reclaimed by Punks as a revolt against the establishment, shredding and repurposing the fabric that once symbolized upper-crust England.

Body piercings

Brightly dyed hair

Band T-shirt

Studded belt

O-ring drop-chain belt

Fishnet stockings

Dr. Martens boots

Padlock chain
necklace

Dog collar

TRUE PUNK

Studded belt

Ripped jeans

DIY Converse sneakers

Black leather pants

④ Safety pins
These were often used decoratively, or to hold ripped clothes together; the pins signified resourcefulness and a rejection of traditional fashion norms.

⑤ Slogan T-shirt
Often featuring bold, provocative messages, slogan tees turned fashion into a political platform, reflecting Punk's activist spirit.

⑥ "Destroy" T-shirt
The anarchic 1977 T-shirt by Vivienne Westwood—which bore a bold red swastika, Sex Pistols lyrics and the word DESTROY—was a challenge to older generations and a rejection of fascist taboos.

⑦ Cuts/cut-offs
Originally denim or leather jackets with the sleeves cut off, cuts were decorated with studs and badges, and painted with band or political logos.

⑧ Military jacket
Often from surplus stores, military jackets were personalized with political slogans and other Punk-related imagery, transforming a symbol of the establishment into a billboard for self-expression.

Rising up amid social turmoil
The UK's economic recession in the 1970s fueled Punk's rise. High unemployment and social unrest created a perfect environment for its anti-establishment ethos; the rebellious music and defiant fashions became a form of protest and expression.

***Never Mind the Bollocks, Here's the Sex Pistols* (1977)**
This seminal work of Punk music is aggressive, anti-establishment and embodies the raw energy and defiance of the era.

"God Save the
Queen" T-shirt (1977)

The godmother of Punk
Vivienne Westwood challenged norms with unconventional and provocative designs. One of her most iconic designs was the "God Save the Queen" T-shirt, a direct critique of the British monarchy and the establishment.

Goths

Goth subculture emerged in the UK during the early 1980s as an offshoot of the post-punk movement. The term is derived from Gothic, a style of literature and architecture known for its dark, brooding atmosphere and intricate complexity.

Release the bats

The Goth subculture started with fans of Gothic rock, an evolution of the post-punk genre characterized by dark, introspective lyrics and a haunting, atmospheric sound. Bands like Bauhaus, Siouxsie and the Banshees, and The Cure played pivotal roles in its formation. The subculture was a response to societal norms, embodying feelings of alienation and the darker aspects of human experience—hence the emphasis on themes of romance, morbidity and existentialism.

Dress code

Goth fashion is characterized by dark clothing, often incorporating elements of Victorian, Elizabethan or medieval attire. Key elements include black velvet, lace, leather and corsets. Silver jewelry, often featuring religious or supernatural symbols, is also prevalent.

Spiky/ studded belt

Mini skirt

Black leather pants

Thigh-high boots

Wristbands and choker

Black fishnet top

Band T-shirt

① Bondage trousers
With their straps and chains, bondage trousers, borrowed from Punk fashion, are popular for their edgy, rebellious aesthetic.

② Winklepickers
These pointy-toed boots or shoes, often made of black leather or suede, have their roots in the 1950s. They were adopted by Goths due to their association with the UK's New Wave scene.

③ Long black coat
Often made from velvet or leather, long coats provide a dramatic, sweeping silhouette and are associated with classic horror and noir films.

④ Silver jewelry
Jewelry often features religious, supernatural, or macabre symbols like crosses, ankhs or skulls.

⑤ Black platform boots
These boots often feature buckles, chains or other metallic details, and are popular for their strong visual statement.

⑥ Corset
Borrowing from Victorian fashion, corsets are popular for their historical associations and their ability to accentuate the body's silhouette.

⑦ Black lace blouse
This historically influenced classic style is popular for its connection to Victorian and Edwardian fashion.

Horror fiction
Bram Stoker's *Dracula's* (1897) darkly atmospheric setting, exploration of the supernatural, and the allure of the immortal yet tormented vampire figure aligns with Goth subculture's fascination with darkness and the macabre.

The Batcave
A London nightclub that opened in 1982, the Batcave was the epicenter of the burgeoning Goth scene. Its dark, mysterious ambience and Gothic rock music helped shape the aesthetics and music of the subculture.

Non-gendered expression
Goth make-up is a form of self-expression that defies traditional gender norms. Dark, dramatic looks featuring black eyeliner, bold lips and pale skin are popular among both male and female Goths.

Bauhaus, *Mask* (1981)

Rivetheads

Fans of industrial music, Rivetheads are characterized by a dystopian, military and industrial aesthetic. The word "rivet" refers to a factory line, and suggests an affinity between harsh sounds and heavy industry.

Fetish-inspired accessories

Mohawk

The sound of dystopia

In the late 1970s, Europe was dealing with social upheaval, including the threat of nuclear war and the rise of neoliberalism; for many Rivetheads, these were a source of dystopianism. Some musicians responded with lyrics that were politically charged, and with an aggressive electronic sound that expressed a sense of anger, frustration and alienation. Throbbing Gristle, a pioneering English industrial band known for experimental sounds and disturbing imagery, helped lay the foundation of Rivethead culture.

Aviator sunglasses

Black military/ biker jacket

Short vinyl skirt

Dress code

The overall style is a combination of industrial, military, Punk and fetish wear. Dark, often leather, clothing is paired with bondage elements and military gear, including jackets, uniforms, tanker boots and metal hardware.

Fingerless gloves

Camouflage

Platform boots with metal hardware

Punk-inspired zipper details

Heavy boots
Such as tanker or combat boots.

Front 242, *Front by Front* (1988)

Black Metal

Black Metal got its name from a genre of extreme heavy metal music. The term was first used in the early 1980s to describe metal bands with satanic lyrics and imagery.

Hail Satan

Black Metal emerged in the 1980s, originating in England and Scandinavia, particularly Norway. Disillusioned with society, the subculture's pioneers sought to create a darker, more extreme form of metal. Rooted in anti-Christian sentiment, the subculture drew on occult and pagan imagery. Black Metal bands emphasized an atmosphere of darkness and evil through low-fi production, tremolo picking and shrieking vocals. The genre gained notoriety for its association with church burnings, violence and criminal activities, which further solidified its rebellious image.

Dress code

Clothes are 100% black, and often include leather, spikes and inverted crosses. Band logos and pagan symbols are also common. Make-up is often corpse paint (black and white). The look is meant to be threatening and rebellious, and reflect a penchant for darkness.

Inverted cross/ pentagram

Long hair

Spiked choker

Band T-shirt

Black leather jacket

Bullet belt

Black leather pants

Spiked wristband

Combat boots

Welcome to Hell (1981)

English band Venom's first albums, *Welcome to Hell* (1981) and *Black Metal* (1982), are often said to be the first Black Metal records.

Psychobillies

Psychobilly combined elements of Punk, rockabilly, and horror. The term is a portmanteau combining "psycho" and "rockabilly," highlighting its eccentric blend of music, fashion and attitude.

Gory rockabillies

The youth subculture known as Psychobilly emerged in the late 1970s and early 1980s in the UK. It was a fusion of Punk rock's raw energy with the rockabilly aesthetic. The music often features fast-paced beats, prominent use of the double bass, and dark, horror-themed lyrics, drawing inspiration from classic horror films and vintage Americana. Early adopters of the subculture were influenced by rockabilly stars including Elvis Presley and Gene Vincent, and the pin-up aesthetic of the 1950s.

Dress code

Psychobilly combined Punk and rockabilly elements with a vintage twist. Key features included leather jackets, band T-shirts, and vintage-inspired dresses. Tattoos, piercings and horror-inspired accessories, such as skull rings, were also popular.

❶ Pencil skirt/dress
Inspired by female Greasers, Psychobillies would wear tight-fitting dresses for a vintage hourglass look.

Black shirt/
band T-shirt

Halter neck

❶

Dr. Martens
boots

High heels

Bleached/
black skinny jeans

Leather
cigarette pants

Flowers/
bows

Studded belt

Brothel creepers

2 DIY leather jacket
Leather jackets were personalized:
usually painted with horror, music and
retro-themed designs, and decorated
with metal studs and spikes.

3 Animal prints
Leopard and zebra print were
popular on clothing and accessories,
inspired by the vintage rock and Glam
styles of the 1950s, and the wild and
uninhibited nature of their music.

4 Printed T-shirt
These mostly black tees usually
featured horror-themed designs and
retro imagery. Popular motifs include
skulls, zombies, pin-up girls and
classic cars.

5 Musical instruments
Psychobilly artists would decorate
their musical instruments with horror,
retro and rockabilly-themed motifs.

6 Bandanna
Inspired by rockabilly, a bandanna was
often tied over Psychobillies' black hair.

The Texas Chainsaw Massacre (1974)
This film is often cited as a major influence on the
Psychobilly scene, with its gritty, visceral
depiction of a cannibalistic family in rural Texas.

Vintage cars
Psychobillies had a strong association with classic
American cars from the 1950s, including Cadillacs,
Chevrolets and custom hot rods.

Psycho ink
Tattoos were used to express
a love of Psychobilly music and
culture. Usually applied on arms and
shoulders, tattoos often featured
horror-themed designs like skulls and
zombies as well as classic Americana
and pin-up imagery.

Harajuku: The Style Epicenter

From a military base to a microtrend mecca, Tokyo's Harajuku district is a celebration of individuality and a beacon for creatives worldwide. Its fusion of traditional and contemporary aesthetics, deeply rooted in Japanese culture, marks Harajuku as a uniquely Japanese fashion phenomenon.

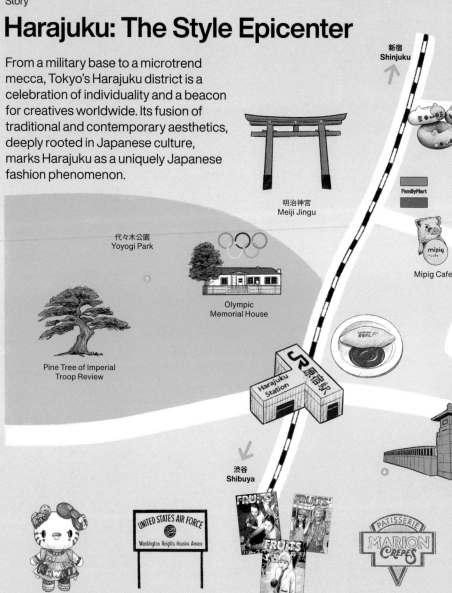

新宿
Shinjuku

明治神宮
Meiji Jingu

FamilyMart

mipig
cafe

Mipig Cafe

代々木公園
Yoyogi Park

Olympic
Memorial House

Pine Tree of Imperial
Troop Review

JR 原宿駅
Harajuku
Station

渋谷
Shibuya

UNITED STATES AIR FORCE
Washington Heights Housing Annex

FRUiTS

PATISSERIE
MARION
CREPES

❶ *Kawaii*—the cult of cuteness

Kawaii means "cute" or "lovable" in Japanese. With its emphasis on all things comforting, nostalgic and non-threatening, Kawaii provides an escape from daily pressures.

❶ Washington Heights

Now Yoyogi Park, this area was a US military housing complex after WWII. Later, it was a village for the 1964 Summer Olympics. This transformation introduced Western culture into the neighborhood, leaving a lasting impact.

❸ FRUiTS magazine

Launched by photographer Shoichi Aoki in 1997, *FRUiTS* published street snaps of Harajuku's creatively dressed young people.

❷ Marion Crepes

The patisserie's founder, Iwao Kishi, drew inspiration from his travels in Europe and brought French-style crepes to Harajuku in 1976.

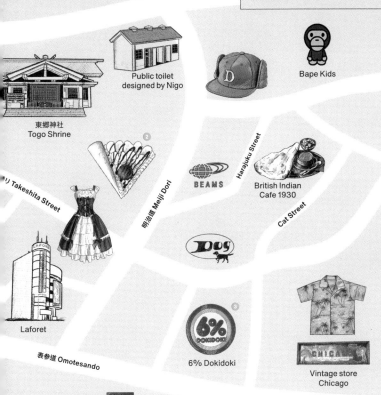

Where is Harajuku?

Tokyo's Harajuku district (原宿) is nestled between the Shinjuku (新宿) and Shibuya wards (渋谷区)—specifically in areas like Takeshita Street (竹下通り), Omotesando (表参道) and Cat Street.

Public toilet designed by Nigo

Bape Kids

東郷神社
Togo Shrine

リ Takeshita Street

明治通 Meiji Dori

Harajuku Street

BEAMS

British Indian Cafe 1930

Cat Street

Dog

Laforet

6%
DOKIDOKI

6% Dokidoki

CHICAGO

Vintage store Chicago

表参道 Omotesando

KIDDY LAND

Rei Kawakubo, one of the original Mansion Makers

③ 6% Dokidoki
This avant-garde fashion boutique is known for loud, colorful styles. Its clothing is popular with international pop stars, including Nicki Minaj and Blackpink.

① 1960–70s: Mansion Makers
Young designers known as "Mansion Makers" set up ateliers in small apartments in the backstreets of Harajuku as well as shops on Takeshita Street.

① 1950s: Omotesando Central Apartments
Initially built for the US military, the complex later attracted a group of fashion creatives, who established themselves there.

④ 1977: Harajuku Hokoten (ホコ天)
From 1997 to 1998, a section of Harajuku's Jingu bridge (神宮橋) was closed to traffic on Sundays; this attracted crowds of performers as well as those who came to showcase their creative clothing styles.

Takenoko-zoku

The *Takenoko-zoku* (竹の子族, "bamboo shoot tribe") was a vibrant Japanese subculture that emerged in the late 1970s. It was known for its unique fashions and frequent gatherings in a popular shopping district in Tokyo.

Eclectic street dancers

The unique subculture started among disaffected youth who embraced new cultural elements but rejected traditional Japanese social norms. It mainly grew around the Harajuku district in Tokyo, where people danced together in streets and in Yoyogi Park, showcasing their unique moves and style. Members took inspiration from various sources, including Western cultural influences and traditional Japanese styles. Their colorful look and eclectic dance moves attracted media attention, giving rise to their widespread popularity.

Dress code

Takenoko-zoku members were known for their flamboyant and colorful outfits, often inspired by anime, manga and other elements of Japanese pop culture. Key features included brightly colored costumes in shiny or metallic materials, and layered accessories.

❶ Bright harem suit
Jumpsuits with baggy harem pants made from shiny, bright-colored synthetic material were part of the look. They were inspired by anime and manga costumes.

Cape

Beaded necklace

Scarf belt

Kung-fu shoes

Leopard pattern

Feather boa

Parachute/
harem pants

2 Uwabaki
Uwabaki are Japanese school slippers, usually worn indoors.

3 Headpiece
Hats and fascinators in various shapes, colors and materials feature unique embellishments; they are sometimes adorned with toys or other novelty items.

4 Marshalling whistle
This can be used to signal different dance moves, to maintain synchronization among the dancers. It could also be used to attract a crowd for a performance.

5 Oversized sunglasses
Often brightly colored and in a retro style, the glasses were sometimes worn with the lenses flipped up.

6 Stuffed toy
Toys, including the famous character Doraemon, were fastened to clothes as an accessory.

7 Boombox
The classic portable stereo system was used to play music for street performances.

8 Haori
A *haori* is a modified kimono-style jacket. It comes in flashy colors and shiny materials.

Eclectic music
Takenoko-zoku music tastes were eclectic, and reflected their wide range of interests, including Western pop (Bee Gees, Abba), Disco (Donna Summer, Village People), and Japanese bands (Pink Lady, Yellow Magic Orchestra).

Theatrical make-up
Both boys and girls wore exaggerated eyeliner, bright lips and heavy contouring that highlighted the cheekbones.

Public group performances
Takenoko-zoku dance routines were fast-paced, upbeat and eclectic, blending Disco, traditional Japanese dance and contemporary Western styles. Members synchronized their movements in energetic group performances.

Karasu-zoku

Karasu-zoku (カラス族) emerged in the late 1980s; the name, meaning "crow tribe," comes from their predominantly black clothing.

Into the darkness

The *Karasu-zoku* subculture originated as a reaction against the bright and flashy fashion and burgeoning *kawaii* (cute) aesthetic in Japan. Young people who identified with Karasu-zoku sought an alternative to mainstream fashion, embracing a darker, more subdued aesthetic. Influenced by Goth, Punk and rock music, as well as designers such as Yohji Yamamoto and Rei Kawakubo of Comme des Garçons, who championed dark, deconstructed and avant-garde clothing, the subculture became a symbol of rebellion and nonconformity for disenchanted Japanese youth.

Dress code

The overall style emphasized a dark, moody and rebellious aesthetic. It typically consisted of loose-fitting black clothing, including jackets, pants and skirts, paired with jet-black hairstyles and pale, neutral make-up.

Straight, sleek hair with choppy bangs

Black stole

Long coat/ collared cape

Ankle-length baggy skirt/pants

Comme des Garçons ad (1981/1998)

Genderless attire

Karasu-zoku fashion was notable for its genderless, figure-hiding approach. Loose-fitting garments and unisex designs blurred the lines between male and female, emphasizing a rejection of traditional gender norms and societal expectations.

Visual Kei

Visual Kei (ヴィジュアル系, "visual style")
was a subculture and musical movement that
emerged in the 1980s. Its name was derived
from the elaborate, theatrical fashion and stage
presence associated with the genre's bands.

Japan rocks

Visual Kei originated in the vibrant
Japanese rock music scene.
Inspired by Western Glam rock
and metal, bands like X Japan and
Buck-Tick adopted flamboyant
styles to set themselves apart.
The movement quickly gained
popularity, as fans embraced
both the music and the striking,
androgynous fashion. Over time,
Visual Kei became synonymous
with a rebellious and avant-
garde attitude, transcending
its musical roots to influence
broader Japanese fashion and
youth culture.

Dress code

Visual Kei was characterized
by elaborate and dramatic
clothing, bold make-up, and
striking hairstyles. Theatrical
garments often incorporated
leather, frills and unconventional
silhouettes. Make-up featured
heavy eyeliner and colorful
eye shadow, while hair was
dyed vibrant colors and styled
in gravity-defying spikes and
intricate braids.

Voluminous,
spiky hair

Dramatic stage
make-up

Piercing

Silver jewelry

Theatrical
costume

Platform boots

X JAPAN
One of the most iconic
bands in the history of Visual
Kei, X Japan's innovative and
pioneering approach to music
and performance combined
elements of heavy metal,
classical and pop. The highly
emotional live performances
set a standard for other
Visual Kei bands to follow.

Lolitas

Lolita subculture draws inspiration from Victorian and Rococo aesthetics while channeling a youthful innocence and coquettishness reminiscent of the title character in Vladimir Nabokov's 1955 novel *Lolita*.

Escape to the past

Lolita fashion emerged as a resistance to Japan's rigid social expectations and the pressures of conformity. It was a reaction to the sexualization and casualness of contemporary Western styles. Emulating the modesty, elegance and intricate detail of the 18th-century Rococo period and the 19th-century Victorian era, it embraced a doll-like aesthetic, celebrating innocence. Starting in Tokyo's Harajuku district, Lolita evolved into various sub-styles, becoming a prominent global influence in alternative fashion circles.

Dress code

Lolitas emphasize modesty, with dresses typically knee-length and worn with bloomers. The style includes petticoats for volume, lace-trimmed blouses, knee-high socks and Mary Jane shoes. Accessories often feature bows, bonnets and parasols, complementing the elaborate feminine aesthetic.

⊕ JSK (jumper skirt)
A jumper skirt is a sleeveless dress that is meant to be worn over a blouse or other top.

Mini hat

Cameo brooch

Blouse

SK (Skirt)

Lace stockings

Walking cane

Rocking horse shoes

Classic Lolita has an elegant vintage look; dresses are often calf length.

Baby, the Stars Shine Bright
One of the oldest and most established Lolita apparel brands, Baby, the Stars Shine Bright is known for its sophisticated, elegant designs and high-quality clothing.

Petticoat etiquette
It is an unwritten rule among Lolitas that petticoats or undergarments should not be visible. It would be a sign of immodesty and carelessness.

Bonnet

Headdress

OP dress
(one-piece dress)

JSK
(jumper skirt)

Petticoat

Platform boots

Gothic Lolita has a black theme, often inspired by Goth and Visual Kei.

Parasol

Tea-party shoes

Sweet Lolita has a cute vibe, with pastel colors, fantasy or childish motifs, and often shorter hemlines.

Tea party
A tea party is social event that allows Lolita enthusiasts to dress up and socialize. It is inspired by Victorian aristocrats and ladies, who would dress up according to a theme and enjoy afternoon tea together.

Gyaru

Gyaru (ギャル) emerged in the Shibuya district of Tokyo. The term comes from the English word "gal," and refers to carefree, stylish young women.

Challenging traditional beauty

Gyaru started as a reaction against traditional Japanese beauty standards of pale skin and dark hair. Young women sought to create their own unique identity, heavily influenced by American fashion and pop culture, with styles like mini skirts, plunging necklines and bronzed skin. The movement gained popularity through magazines like *Egg* and *Popteen*, which showcased Gyaru styles. The Shibuya district of Tokyo, particularly the famous Shibuya 109 shopping center, became the epicenter of this subculture.

Dress code

There are many sub-groups under Gyaru. The fashion is generally characterized by *kawaii* (cute) yet daring styles and layers of accessories. Key elements include mini skirts, platform shoes, colorful nails, dyed hair and eye-catching make-up.

❶ Oversized cardigan
Worn over mini skirts, the cardigan's sleeves cover most of the hands to create an innocent look.

❷ Bubble socks
These oversized, baggy socks are often worn with school uniforms and paired with platform shoes.

Tanned skin

Gyaru peace sign
A reverse-V hand gesture that expresses peace, fun and friendship.

Fur leg warmers

Kogal—A high-school Gyaru

Agejo—A mature, glamorous Gyaru

Mini skirt/shorts

Furry ear muffs

Fur boots

③ Frilly mini dress
Super-short dresses, sometimes pleated or ruffled, emphasize the legs and create a youthful, flirtatious look.

④ Platform shoes
Platform shoes, especially boots, add height, create a dramatic silhouette, and are often adorned with decorations such as fur, chains or buckles.

⑤ Bold accessories
Statement-making accessories, such as layered necklaces and chunky bracelets, add a sense of playfulness and personalization.

⑥ Intricate nail art
Nail extensions feature elaborate designs, rhinestones and other 3D decorations.

⑦ Heavily decorated mobile phone
Flip phones are usually decorated with copious rhinestones, cute stickers and charms.

⑧ Faux-fur coat
These jackets, vests and accessories add a touch of luxury and glamour to Gyaru outfits.

Namie Amuro
Often credited with popularizing the Gyaru subculture in the mid-1990s. Namie Amuro had tanned skin and bleached hair. She helped establish the Gyaru look as a mainstream fashion trend in Japan.

Namie Amuro, Genius (2000)

Photo stickers
Stickers known as *purikura* are popular among Gyaru. Purikura machines allow users to take photos and decorate them with cute graphics and filters. The stickers are often kept as mementos.

Dolly eyes
Heavy eye make-up creates a doll-like look with lots of eyeliner and eye shadow, and extensive false lashes.

Types of Gyaru
Influenced by other subcultures, Gyaru has developed into different sub-styles:

Agejo	Glamorous and sensual
B-Kei	Hip-Hop and R&B-inspired
Himegyaru	All-pink princess
Kogal	High-school-girl inspired
Rokku	Rock and Goth
Yamanba	Hawaiian-themed, with extreme tan

Decora Kei

Decora Kei (デコラ系) is a vibrant, colorful street-fashion style. The name "decora" is derived from the word "decoration," reflecting the style's emphasis on layering accessories and clothing.

Chasing rainbows

Decora Kei emerged in the late 1990s in Harajuku, the Tokyo district known for its eclectic fashion scene; the subculture was a response to the minimalist and monochromatic styles that dominated Japanese fashion. Decora Kei sought to break free from these constraints and embrace bold, eye-catching colors and patterns reminiscent of children's clothing, drawing inspiration from *kawaii* culture's emphasis on cuteness and innocence. The playful aesthetic allows for individuality and creativity. The style has a dedicated following that continues to thrive today.

Dress code

Decora Kei style is characterized by childlike bright colors, patterns and layers. Outfits often include multiple layers of clothing, such as skirts over pants, and excessive use of accessories like hair clips, bracelets, necklaces and leg warmers.

❶ Cartoon characters
Enthusiasts often attach characters—in the form of patches, charms and even plush toys—to their clothing and accessories to create a fun and playful look.

❷ Tulle skirt
Layered tulle skirts come in bright colors, and may feature additional decorative elements such as lace, ribbons or appliqués.

Rainbow colors

Colorful socks

Puffer jacket

Kids' backpack

Hair clips

Suspender skirt

3 Leg warmers
Adding to the overall layered look, leg warmers often have fun motifs, such as smiley faces and rainbows.

4 Plush bag
Bags and backpacks are designed like a stuffed animal or toy. This adds extra childishness and a sense of play to the style.

5 Plastic accessories
Brightly colored, kawaii-inspired plastic-bead necklaces, bracelets and rings are often layered.

6 Platform shoes
These range from sneakers to boots, and often feature bold colors, prints and decorative elements like buckles, chains or charms.

7 Face stickers
Stickers of hearts, stars or smiley faces may replace make-up, and are sometimes also used as adhesive bandages.

DIY culture
Decora Kei enthusiasts often make their own accessories from plastic beads, charms and toys, since fashion stores may not satisfy their unique style requirements. The subculture champions do-it-yourself creativity, emphasizing individuality and resourcefulness while celebrating their signature style.

Rainbow hair
Elaborate hairstyles, including braids, buns or pigtails, are often dyed in vivid hues and styled with bows, ribbons and clips.

Tomoe Shinohara
The origins of Decora Kei fashion can be traced back to Japanese idol Tomoe Shinohara's style. Her fans, called "Shinora," emulated her look with excessive hair clips and childish accessories.

Fairy Kei

A whimsical Japanese street style, *Fairy Kei* (フェアリー系) translates to "fairy-style" and embodies the subculture's fascination with pastel colors, nostalgic motifs and childlike innocence.

Fairyland fantasies

Fairy Kei emerged in the 2000s, drawing inspiration from 1980s and 1990s pop culture, including toys such as My Little Pony and animated TV series such as *Rainbow Brite*. This nostalgic, dreamy style resonated with those seeking a delicate aesthetic, characterized by pastel colors, fantasy motifs and an idealized vision of Western childhood. Popularized in Tokyo's Harajuku district, Fairy Kei gained traction among young people who appreciated its playful, youthful charm and connection to childhood memories.

Dress code

Characterized by pastel colors, ruffles and lace, Fairy Kei fashion incorporates items such as oversized sweaters, puffy skirts and knee-high socks. Accessories often feature plush toys, bows and heart motifs, contributing to the style's whimsical nature.

Ribbon hair clips

Pink hair

Oversized sweater

A-line dress

Cartoon bag/toy

Tulle skirt

Pastel tights

Care Bears
Care Bears were created by American Greetings in 1981. They are known for their belly badges, which represent their personalities and powers.

Mori Kei

Mori Kei (森系), or "forest style," is characterized by earthy, whimsical fashions. The lifestyle embraces nature, simplicity and a slower pace of living.

Back to nature
Mori Kei emerged in the mid-2000s as a reaction to fast-paced, consumer-driven society, and expressed a desire to reconnect with the serenity and beauty of the natural world. The style and lifestyle are deeply rooted in the forest and nature, drawing inspiration from woodland creatures, enchanting landscapes and the tranquility found in secluded groves. Mori Kei gained traction through online communities and social-media platforms, where members shared their earthy outfits, DIY projects, and love of the great outdoors.

Dress code
The style incorporates loose, layered clothing made from natural fibers including cotton, linen and wool in earthy colors, with occasional floral patterns. Accessories include handmade items such as crocheted pieces and nature-inspired jewelry.

Crochet/ lace

Scarf/ shawl

Sweater vest

Warm socks

Bulky sweater

Layered fabrics

Lace-up leather boots/ hiking boots

Mori boy

Mori girl

Dot-com boom

Globalization

Alternative Goes Mainstream

Marked by the end of the Cold War and the dawn of the digital age, the 1990s ushered in a dramatic transformation in fashion. The era saw a shift toward alternative styles, the mass adoption of trends fueled by celebrity culture, and a mainstream integration of street-inspired fashion, reflecting the decade's dynamic socio-cultural shifts.

The golden age of Supermodels

Introduction of diffusion lines

Friends (1994–2004)

ICQ (1996)

Minimalism

This fashion movement emerged during the 1990s.
Its name is derived from the aesthetic, which focuses on
simplicity, clean lines and a less-is-more approach.

Less is more
Minimalism was a reaction to the
bold, extravagant fashion trends
of the 1980s. As society moved
away from the excesses and
materialism of the previous
decade, designers and consumers
sought a more pared-down,
functional aesthetic. The
movement was heavily influenced
by designers including Calvin
Klein, Helmut Lang and
Jil Sander. Their collections were
characterized by monochrome
palettes, high-quality materials,
and an emphasis on comfort
and practicality.

Dress code
The look included simple tailored
pieces such as slip dresses,
oversized blazers and straight-
leg pants. Key elements were
monochromatic and androgynous
outfits, subdued colors, and
a focus on quality. Accessories
were understated.

❶ White top
Structured woven shirts, simple
tank tops and fitted T-shirts were
simple yet refined, featuring
clean lines and no embellishment.

❷ Straight-leg jeans
High-waisted, straight-leg
jeans were popular for simplicity and
comfort. Often made from high-
quality denim, they could be paired
with cropped tops.

❸ Slip dress
This minimalist staple featured a
simple, form-fitting silhouette with
spaghetti straps, and was often
made from silk or satin. The dress was
popular for its effortless elegance
and versatility.

Leather
boots

Strappy
sandals

Vest

Tailored pants

Oval sunglasses

Tank top

④ Button-up shirt
A boxy shirt with a straight hemline created a loose and comfortable fit; it was often worn with only the third and fourth buttons fastened.

⑤ Oversized blazer
Loose-fitting blazers were popular for their androgynous look.

⑥ Slip skirt
This fluid, straight-cut staple was midi or maxi length.

⑦ Leather mules or slides
Flat or wedge slip-ons without straps were popular for their effortless style.

⑧ Turtleneck sweater
Sleeveless or long-sleeved, the turtleneck created a sleek silhouette that could be layered or worn alone.

The queen of less: Jil Sander
Sander cemented minimalism's prominence in the 1990s. Known for precise tailoring, high-quality fabrics and muted colors, her luxurious yet simple styles made minimalism chic. Like other minimalist designers, Sander rejected logos and let the clothes speak for themselves.

Kate Moss in a Calvin Klein underwear ad (1993)

Heroin chic
The waifish look celebrated thinness and androgyny. It aligned with the minimalist approach, emphasizing simple, understated beauty. It created an alternative to the voluptuous models of the '80s.

Eclectic minimalism
Minimalism took on various nuances, like the conceptual aesthetics of three Japanese designers: Yohji Yamamoto, Rei Kawakubo and Issey Miyake, who view fashion as an expression of deeper meaning, not as a status symbol.

Grunge

Grunge subculture and style emerged in the late '80s and was heavily influenced by the Seattle music scene of the same name. The name comes from the word "grungy," which means dirty or unkempt.

Anti-fashion fashion
Originating in Seattle, Grunge was a response to 1980s consumerism and materialism, and reflected the economic decline of the region. Bands like Nirvana, Pearl Jam and Soundgarden embraced this counterculture, creating music with dark, angst-filled themes. Grunge's gritty, rebellious sound influenced the dress and attitude of its fans. Flannel shirts, ripped jeans and thrift-store clothing were a rejection of the clean-cut pop culture of the 1980s, and matched the anti-establishment ethos of the music scene.

Dress code
Clothes were often worn and faded; layering them exuded a casual and low-maintenance attitude. Key elements included thrift-store items such as grandpa cardigans, flannel shirts, ripped jeans, combat boots and knitted hats.

❶ Flannel shirt
A staple of grunge fashion, plaid flannel shirts were worn loose or tied around the waist for a laid-back, anti-establishment attitude.

❷ Ripped jeans
Distressed denim, often with frayed holes and tears, reflected the gritty, rebellious nature of Grunge music and culture.

Choker

Denim jacket

Ripped tights

Converse sneakers

③ Floral dress
Floral prints added a soft, feminine element to the look; they ranged from mini to maxi in length, and were often paired with oversized flannel shirts or cardigans.

Midi skirt

Slouchy beanie

Cut-offs

Vintage military jacket

④ Band T-shirt
Oversized tees featuring the logos or artwork of grunge bands showcased fans' musical preferences.

⑤ Dr. Martens boots
These sturdy lace-up boots were popular for their practicality and durability.

⑥ Grandpa sweater
Baggy, worn-out sweaters and cardigans contributed to the thrift-store-chic aesthetic and demonstrated a rejection of mainstream fashion trends.

Soundgarden, *Superunknown* (1994)

Grunge music
Characterized by raw, distorted guitars and introspective lyrics, Grunge music emerged from the Pacific Northwest underground scene.

High-fashion rebel
Marc Jacobs revolutionized high fashion by embracing Grunge aesthetics, melding edgy streetwear with luxury elements. The boundary-breaking designs transformed Grunge from a subculture to a global phenomenon.

Kurt Cobain in *The Face*, September 1993

Kurt Cobain
The Nirvana front man's influence transcended music; fans and fashion enthusiasts alike were drawn to the authenticity and rebellious spirit of his style. His effortless, anti-materialistic approach to fashion was emblematic of the aesthetic.

Kinderwhore

Popularized by Grunge singer/songwriters including Courtney Love, the Kinderwhore look was a feminist statement intended to subvert traditional Western standards of beauty, youth, "good-girl" innocence and femininity.

Girly meets grungy

Influenced by feminist values, Kinderwhore style was a response to the hypersexualization of women and a rejection of mainstream beauty standards. By intentionally twisting, destroying, and even sexualizing a traditional good-girl look in a dramatic way, Kinderwhore aimed to create a shocking and confrontational visual contradiction, and to comment on the objectification of women.

Dress code

A messy yet girlish look, Kinderwhore was a combination of innocence and Grunge edginess. Staples included baby-doll dresses with torn stockings and combat boots or Mary Janes. Vintage princessy accessories including tiaras and heart-locket pendants were often paired with chokers and chains.

Scruffy hair

Smoky eyes/ smudged eyeliner

Glamorous jewelry

Red lips

Fur/ faux-fur coat

Lace/ ruffles

Fishnet tights

Mary Janes

Kat Bjelland
The lead singer of Babes in Toyland is widely believed to be the first to establish and wear the Kinderwhore style. It was later popularized by her roommate, Courtney Love.

Riot Grrrl

Riot Grrrl subculture emerged in the early 1990s as an underground feminist Punk movement, primarily in the Pacific Northwest. "Grrrl" stands for both "girl" and a growling sound, emphasizing female empowerment, defiance and anger.

Punk's feminist uprising

Riot Grrrl was a response to the male-dominated Punk scene and a cultural climate that often dismissed or marginalized women's voices. Bands including Bikini Kill, Bratmobile and Heavens to Betsy sought to challenge the patriarchy and sexism, and provided platforms for female voices through zines and events. The movement was considered a major catalyst for the third wave of feminism, which was more diverse and more inclusive of women from different backgrounds.

Dress code

Riot Grrrl fashion was a girly offshoot of Punk. Staples included band T-shirts or baby tees, plaid skirts or pants, schoolgirl skirts, and combat boots or Mary Janes. Outfits often incorporated messages on patches, buttons and tees, emphasizing the scene's activist roots.

Body graffiti
The body was seen as a canvas for personal or political statements.

Bright-colored/ bleached hair

Ringer T-shirt

Choker

Shift dress

Plaid/tartan mini skirt

White socks

Dr. Martens boots

Converse sneakers

Political and band pins

Street Skaters

Street Skaters skateboard in public places.
They pride themselves on skating creatively and
using the city as a playground.

The urban playground

Street skating originated in the
1980s but grew into a full-fledged
subculture in the 1990s. It started
in major cities like Los Angeles,
New York and San Francisco as
a reaction to the decline of skate
parks. Young skaters started
exploring city streets and using
architectural elements like stairs,
handrails, curbs and benches.
Videos by companies like Blind
Skateboards popularized the
styles and fashions, providing
a sense of belonging and
identity for adventurous urban
kids who felt alienated from the
mainstream.

Dress code

Influenced by Punk, Grunge
and Hip-Hop styles, skater
attire focuses on comfort and
practicality. Key elements
include baggy pants, oversized
graphic tees featuring skate
brands, and shoes such as
Vans or Airwalks.

❶ Beanie
Good for keeping hair back when
performing tricks, beanies also keep
the head warm in colder weather.

❷ Flannel shirt
Demonstrating the Grunge
influence on skater fashion, flannel
shirts are often worn unbuttoned
and layered over T-shirts.

❸ Cargo pants
These loose-fitting pants conceal
knee pads, and are comfortable and
roomy enough for skating; the extra
pockets are great for stashing
belongings.

Hoodie

Long-sleeved T-shirt

VHS skateboarding videos

Airwalk Ones

Cargo shorts

4 Oversized graphic T-shirt
Tees feature logos, designs or slogans from brands like Thrasher, Spitfire and Independent.

5 Baggy jeans
A staple of skater fashion, baggy jeans allow comfort and freedom of movement. Brands like JNCO and Etnies feature wide legs and relaxed fits.

6 High-top sneakers
These sneakers provide ankle support and protection. Popular choices include Vans Sk8-Hi, Airwalk, and Converse Chuck Taylors.

7 Snapback cap
Often worn backwards, these hats might show team logos or skate brand insignias.

8 Personalized skateboard
Skateboards can be personalized with stickers, grip tape, custom graphics and painted decks to express style and individuality.

9 Crew socks
Often striped and branded, these socks are pulled up high, and complement baggy jeans and skate shoes.

Park vs street
Park skating emphasizes ramps and bowls for high speed and aerial tricks; street skating focuses on creativity, adaptability and interaction with urban elements such as stairs, handrails and curbs, which facilitate technical flips, grinds and slides.

The Original Vans: #44 Deck Shoes

Iconic brand
Originating in Anaheim, California in 1966, Vans became popular among Southern California skateboarders and surfers.

Thrasher, July 1990

Skateboarding magazines
Major skateboarding magazines including Thrasher, Transworld Skateboarding and Big Brother popularized the subculture.

Extreme Games 1995
The X Games debuted in Newport in 1995, bringing skateboarding into the mainstream and inspiring amateurs.

Roller Skaters

Roller skating has been a popular pastime and sport for many years. The roller-skater subculture of the 1990s was born from a fusion of skateboarding and rollerblading as well as a love of music and dance.

Freedom on wheels

Rollerblades, also known as inline skates, revolutionized roller-skating culture in the 1990s, providing greater speed and agility. Urban streets, parks and parking lots became havens for skaters to showcase their tricks and jumps. Pioneers such as Arlo Eisenberg and Chris Edwards popularized aggressive inline skating, inspiring a new generation to express themselves through movement. Skate parties became popular social events. Celebrating the roller-skating community, these parties featured themed nights, contests and showcases, appealing to those seeking a carefree form of recreation and escape.

Dress code

Emphasizing athletic and streetwear designs, the style prioritized comfort and functionality. Baggy pants, bold graphics, bright colors and accessories such as baseball caps and wristbands were also popular.

❶ Cropped top
Female roller skaters often wore crop tops, usually in bright colors; this allowed them to show off their midriff.

❷ Dolphin shorts
These nylon sports shorts had contrasting trim and rounded side slits.

❸ Oversized T-shirt
Skateboarding and roller-skating culture often intersected, and skate-brand T-shirts were a popular choice for roller skaters. The oversized fit allowed ease of movement.

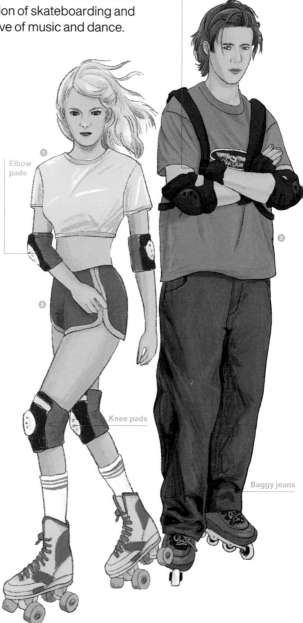

Wrist guards

Elbow pads

❶

❷

Knee pads

❸

Baggy jeans

Biker shorts

④

Baseball cap

⑥

Helmet

Slap wristbands

⑤

Track pants

⑦

④ Bikini top
Often seen on beachfront skaters, these tops come in bright colors and bold graphic patterns.

⑤ Striped tube socks
Typically knee-high or calf-length, these classic socks have stripes at the top. They provide comfort and support for skaters, and add a touch of style.

⑥ Fanny pack
This convenient accessory allows skaters to carry their essentials without the need for a purse or backpack. They are often brightly colored or come in bold patterns.

⑦ Cut-offs
The high waist of this '90s fashion staple provided a comfortable and secure fit while skating. These shorts typically have raw edges and are worn with tucked-in shirts or crop tops.

Hot Skatin' Barbie (1995)
From Mattel's "Cool Times" line, this doll came with a pair of neon-yellow rollerblades, and represented the popularity of rollerblading among girls. The bright outfit reflected and celebrated the fashions of the era.

Airborne (1993)
The movie *Airborne* capitalized on the popularity of rollerblading. It featured rebellious teens bonding over the sport, and showcased flashy stunts.

	Rollerblades (inline skates)	Roller skates
Design	Single frame with 3 to 5 wheels and plastic boots	Wide wheel base with 4 wheels arranged in a square pattern
Characteristics	Super-fast, smooth ride	Quick moves, spins and turns
Use	Commuting, speed skating	Skating parties

Hip-Hop: East Coast

This subgenre of Hip-Hop fashion originated in the northeastern United States. Characterized by its sophisticated and urban look, East Coast Hip-Hop style is often seen as a more lyrical, gritty alternative to West Coast Hip-Hop style.

Beats from the East

The emergence of East Coast Hip-Hop can be traced back to block parties in the Bronx, where DJs like Kool Herc pioneered the art of breakbeat deejaying. The reality of the New York City streets provided the backdrop for the development of this unique style. Combining rhythmic beats, storytelling through rap lyrics, and a focus on local experiences, East Coast Hip-Hop evolved as a powerful medium for self-expression and social commentary among marginalized communities.

Dress code

East Coast Hip-Hop fashion is characterized by baggy jeans, branded clothing and athletic wear. Kangol hats are a popular headwear choice, and are often paired with high-top sneakers, Adidas Superstars and Timberland boots.

❶ Dookie chain
Chunky gold jewelry is a Hip-Hop staple—a symbol of wealth and success. Rope-like chain necklaces often come with a large medallion.

❷ Tracksuit
Usually Adidas or Nike, tracksuits are an extension of B-Boy culture.

Large hoop earrings

Kangol bucket hat

Bandeau top

Adidas Superstar sneakers

Branded sweatshirt

Puffer jacket

Baggy jeans

Leather coat

Starter jacket

Kangol flat cap

Rimless sunglasses

Timberland boots

Two-finger rings

❸ Puffer jacket
Down jackets, particularly those by The North Face and Tommy Hilfiger, were worn oversized and provided warmth during harsh East Coast winters.

❹ Starter jacket
Popular for their high quality and flashy designs, these expensive jackets served as potent status symbols. They often featured team logos, showcasing loyalty to a sports team or city.

❺ Baggy jeans
Characterized by their loose fit and low crotches, baggy jeans were popularized by Girbaud and Tommy Hilfiger.

❻ Kangol flat cap
Popularized by Run-DMC and LL Cool J, these British-made hats were known for their design and their iconic logo.

❼ Timberland boots
Also known as "Timbs," and often worn with laces untied, these tan boots were known for their rugged look and durability. Artists like Notorious B.I.G. and the Wu-Tang Clan popularized them.

Dapper Dan
Harlem-based designer Dapper Dan was hugely influential in Hip-Hop fashion. He pioneered the use of luxury logos on streetwear, including tracksuits and bomber jackets, defining the aesthetic. Although his boutique was shut down due to trademark issues, his impact has endured.

Nas, *Illmatic* (1994)

A challenge to classism
Hip-Hop's embrace of Polo Ralph Lauren fused the brand's aspirational, upper-class lifestyle with the working-class roots of many artists and fans, allowing them to challenge societal norms of wealth and success, and assert their identity.

The art of the diss
Rap battles in New York City featured two rappers facing off with clever putdowns, often in a freestyle format. Artists would showcase their lyrical skills and boast about their accomplishments.

Hip-Hop: West Coast

This subgenre of Hip-Hop fashion originated in the western United States. Characterized by its relaxed fit and gangsta vibe, West Coast Hip-Hop style is often seen as a more melodic, laid-back alternative to East Coast style.

Straight outta Compton

The West Coast Hip-Hop scene was shaped by the sociopolitical climate of Los Angeles—particularly gang culture and street life. Pioneering artists like Ice-T and N.W.A. used rap as a medium to address issues like police brutality, racism and poverty. The music was characterized by its laid-back, funk-influenced beats and explicit lyrics, reflecting the experiences of marginalized communities in the city. As a result, West Coast Hip-Hop became an influential force in both music and social activism.

Dress code

West Coast Hip-Hop fashion is characterized by casual street-gang style, and features baggy khakis, Pendleton shirts, bandannas and sports jerseys. Sneakers are essential, and baseball caps are typically worn backwards or sideways.

❶ Pendleton shirt
Often worn oversized and layered over T-shirts, these classic plaid shirts were popular in the West Coast Hip-Hop scene because of their connections to Chicano and low-rider culture.

❷ Bomber jacket
Oversized jackets customized with patches or embroidery represent sports-team loyalty.

Baseball cap

Large hoop earrings

Baggy jeans

Black jeans

Beanie

Layered
gold chains

Oversized hoodie

Carhartt chore jacket

Overals

❸ Bandanna
Colorful patterned bandannas are often used as headbands. They were appropriated from both gang culture and Chicano fashion.

❹ Coach jacket
These lightweight nylon windbreakers have snap buttons and a shirt-style collar. Major artists such as N.W.A. and Ice Cube customized theirs.

❺ Loc sunglasses
This staple featured dark lenses and a thick, rectangular frame.

❻ Nike Cortez sneakers
Originally designed in 1972 as running shoes, the sneakers gained popularity in Southern California for their comfort, style and affordability.

❼ Khaki pants/shorts
Influenced by Cholos, oversized khakis and cargo pants are a popular choice. The loose fit and utilitarian vibe suit the West Coast lifestyle.

❽ Sports jersey
Football, basketball and baseball jerseys are worn in support of favorite teams or hometowns. They are oversized and are often worn layered with white T-shirts.

Snoop Dogg's custom "Snoop DeVille," a Cadillac low rider

Chicano influence
LA is the mecca of Chicano culture; Cholos inspired the style, popularizing Pendleton shirts, bandannas and low-rider car culture. Gangsta rap lyrics drew heavily from Chicano gang and street culture, incorporating their slang and references.

Doggystyle (1993)
Snoop Dogg's debut album, produced by Dr. Dre, cemented the G-funk sound in West Coast Hip-Hop, and showcased Snoop's laid-back flow and storytelling abilities.

Oakland Raiders
The Raiders are a professional football team based in Oakland, California. Their tough, blue-collar image and embrace of a renegade, outlaw ethos made them popular among fans of Hip-Hop and gangsta rap.

Sneakers Take Center Stage

Although they started out as simple, rubber-soled "plimsolls" in Britain in the 1800s, sneakers have evolved into a worldwide staple of fashion and day-to-day life. Their ubiquity—from streets and schoolyards to the red carpet—is a testament to their metamorphosis into a prominent status symbol.

From the court to the catwalk

Athlete endorsement (1970–80s)
Major sports brands leveraged star athletes to popularize their sneakers. These endorsements elevated the shoes from sports equipment to symbolic fashion, resonating with fans who sought to emulate their heroes.

<u>Left</u>
Puma Clyde (1971)—Endorsed by NBA star Walt "Clyde" Frazier.

<u>Right</u>
Nike Air Jordan (1985)—A collaboration that transformed the sneaker industry.

Musicians as trendsetters (1980s–90s)
Popular musicians wore sneakers, aligning the shoes with influential images of rebellion, individualism and cultural identity.
This transformed sneakers into symbols of different musical genres and youth cultures, transcending their athletic origins.

The origin of the "sneaker"

The term originated from the verb "to sneak," as rubber soles allowed quieter movement than leather soles. The term was popularized in the advertising of Keds by the United Rubber Company in 1917.

The icons

① Converse Chuck Taylor sneakers
→ Released in 1917
→ Endorsed by Chuck Taylor in 1923

The original rules!
Converse attempted to update the shoes in the 1990s by adding comfort features. Loyal fans vehemently protested the changes, and the brand was compelled to continue producing the original model alongside the new versions.

② Adidas Stan Smith
→ Released in 1965
→ Endorsed by & named after Stan Smith in 1978

Adidas Robert Haillet?
Adidas originally named the iconic tennis shoe the Adidas Robert Haillet in 1965, after the famous French tennis player. They renamed the shoe the Adidas Stan Smith in 1978.

③ Nike Air Jordan
→ Released in 1985
→ Endorsed by & named after Michael Jordan

Banned shoes
Nike's black and red Air Jordans violated the NBA's "51% white" rule, and the league fined Jordan $5,000 per game for wearing them. Nike turned the ban into a marketing opportunity, enhancing the sneaker's rebel appeal and popularity.

The crossover to luxury (2000s & beyond)
Collaborations between sneaker brands, celebrities and luxury fashion houses further cemented their status and successfully merged streetwear and luxury, increasing sneakers' popularity—and sales.

Hip-Hop group Run-DMC famously endorsed Adidas Superstars, and released a song called "My Adidas" (1986).

Grunge legend Kurt Cobain was often spotted in Converse Chuck Taylor sneakers.

Fenty Puma Creeper (2015)— a collaboration between Puma and Rihanna.

Dior × Air Jordan 1 (2020)— 8,000 pairs of limited-edition "Air Dior" sneakers were available to the public; 5 million people signed up to buy them.

Juggalos

The Juggalo subculture is a devoted fan base of the horrorcore Hip-Hop duo Insane Clown Posse (ICP). The name comes from the 1992 ICP song "The Juggla," and has since come to define this unique and passionate community.

Clan of the fringe carnie crew

The subculture emerged in the early 1990s when ICP's gritty and violent Hip-Hop style gained a following. Their music incorporated horrorcore themes and a "carnival" motif that resonated with disaffected youth. Followers were attracted to ICP's underdog image and anti-mainstream stance. The band emphasized that Juggalos were like family, and this close-knit community appealed to outcasts and misfits. Their annual gathering of the Juggalos festival and underground concerts helped bring fans together and strengthen the subculture.

Dress code

Juggalo fashion includes oversized jerseys, band merchandise and baggy clothing. Accessories often feature the Hatchetman logo, a symbol of the Dark Carnival, and the ICP logo. Juggalos also incorporate elements of Punk, Goth and Hip-Hop styles.

Clown face paint
Typically black and white, with exaggerated eyebrows and mouth lines.

W.C. (wicked clown) hand sign

Hatchetman logo

Baggy shorts/ pants

Spider-leg hairstyle
Usually worn by women (Juggalettes), the style can be made from braids or dreadlocks.

Sapeurs

This unique fashion movement started in the Congo; the name *Sapeur* comes from the French acronym *SAPE*, meaning "Société des Ambianceurs et des Personnes Élégantes," which translates to "Society of Tastemakers and Elegant People."

Men of panache

Emerging in Kinshasa and Brazzaville after independence from colonial rule, the capitals on opposite banks of the Congo River became centers for new African elites. Gaining prominence in the 1980s and 1990s, Sapeur style allowed Congolese men to showcase wealth and status. Inspired by the European colonialists' attire, Sapeurs asserted dignity and challenged African stereotypes by adopting a stylish and luxurious way of dress. They represented a generation caught between a colonial past and an independent future, clinging to ideals of modernity and mobility.

Dress code

Known for their flamboyant and refined dress sense, Sapeurs wear tailored suits and eye-catching patterns. Accessories such as fedoras, pocket squares and canes or umbrellas are essential to the look.

Bowler hat

Bow tie/tie

Scarf

Bright pocket square

Tailored suit

Cane/ umbrella

Flashy socks

Polished brogues

The king of *La Sape*
World-famous Congolese musician Papa Wemba is known as La Sape's founder and spiritual father.

Cholombianos

Cholombiano is a Mexican youth subculture that emerged in the late 1990s in the working-class suburbs of Monterrey, Mexico. It is known for its slicked-down hairstyle, its love of *cumbia* music, and its strong sense of community.

Cumbia & community

Cholombiano subculture emerged in the late 1990s in the working-class neighborhoods of Monterrey, Mexico, where diverse ethnic and cultural backgrounds intersected. These communities were home to a mix of mestizo and indigenous populations as well as Colombian immigrants, creating a unique cultural blend. Cholombianos were influenced by the fusion of traditional Mexican and Colombian elements, specifically *cumbia* and *vallenato* music. Their multicultural identity allowed them to challenge stereotypes and create an anti-establishment subculture.

Dress code

The blend of Cholo street style and Caribbean elements features oversized clothing in a mix of vibrant colors and patterns. Key items include baggy pants, Hawaiian shirts, and clothing and accessories with religious iconography.

❶ Oversized plaid shirt
Large plaid patterns are often seen on short-sleeved shirts, sometime in a traditional *guayabera* style.

❷ Baseball cap
Cholombianos often wear caps that are too small, so they remain perched on top of the head. Sometimes the caps are airbrushed with personalized messages.

Converse sneakers

Bandanna

Hawaiian shirt

Oversized T-shirt

Nike Cortez sneakers

Baggy Dickies/
Dickies shorts

❸ Rosary beads
The traditional Catholic prayer necklace is worn by Cholombianos as a symbol of their faith.

❹ Oversized T-shirt
Large graphic T-shirts, usually in vibrant colors, feature band logos, religious imagery or pop-culture references.

❺ Escapulario
This traditional Catholic necklace, called a "scapular" in English, is made of fabric or metal and features an image of the Virgin Mary as well as religious inscriptions.

❻ Hand-woven necklace
DIY beaded necklaces are emblazoned with the name of a neighborhood, a favorite radio station or other interests.

❼ Loose-fit cropped pants/shorts
Baggy, cropped pants are worn in bright colors, and sometimes in bold patterns such as giant checks and prints.

❽ Catholic iconography
Shirts often feature prints of Catholic imagery, such as Our Lady of Guadalupe, which reflects Cholombianos' religious beliefs and identity.

Slicked hair
Hair is the most important aspect of the look. Styles often feature long, slicked-down sideburns, a shaved rectangular patch at the back (with a rat tail), and slicked-down bangs in dramatic spikes; the style uses lots of hair gel.

Cliques
Cholombianos have their own small groups. Each group has its own graffiti-style hand signals, which they flash in a dance circle to represent their set.

Cumbia music
Cumbia, a genre born on Colombia's Caribbean coast, mixes African drumming with Spanish melodies. It found its foothold in Mexico mid-century and bred an unprecedented, passionate teen fan base in the 1990s.

El Gran Silencio,
Chuntaro Style (2001)

Ravers

Raver culture grew out of the Acid House music scene in the UK in the late 1980s and early 1990s. The term "rave" refers to all-night dance parties where electronic music was played.

Underground techno therapy

Seeking an escape from everyday life, raves provided a place for young people to party freely after hours. As Acid House music gained in popularity, underground raves transformed into massive commercial events. The subculture quickly spread across Europe and North America. The scene was characterized by underground parties, often held in abandoned warehouses, where DJs would spin electronic dance music such as techno, trance, and drum and bass. Ravers enjoyed a sense of community, freedom and escape from the mainstream.

Dress code

The Raver look reflects a playful and eccentric style, and typically includes neon colors and loose-fitting clothing that is suitable for all-night dancing. Accessories like glow sticks, LED lights and pacifiers are common.

❶ Reflective details
Reflective tape and ink on T-shirts and pants glows under UV black light, creating a neon sea of color at raves. It increases visibility and enhances the psychedelic atmosphere.

Colored sunglasses

Face glitter and jewels

Wide-leg pants

Bikini

Visor

② Glow sticks
Plastic tubes filled with luminescent chemicals are often worn as bracelets or necklaces, creating an otherworldly effect and facilitating visibility in dark clubs.

③ Phat pants
Oversized, wide-leg pants with bold patterns and reflective materials create a visually stimulating effect while dancing.

④ Shutter shades
Futuristic eyewear with tinted lenses and unique designs serve as a statement accessory.

⑤ Kandi accessories
Brightly colored, homemade beaded bracelets, necklaces and cuffs, often featuring phrases or symbols, represent personal beliefs or experiences.

⑥ Pacifier
Originally used to prevent the tooth grinding caused by MDMA, pacifiers became an iconic Raver accessory.

⑦ Crop top
Midriff-baring tops often feature eye-catching patterns and provide a fun, youthful look while allowing for freedom of movement.

⑧ Hydration pack
These keep ravers hydrated as they dance all night.

⑨ Platform sneakers
Big shoes with chunky soles facilitate all-night dancing; they come in many designs and styles.

P.L.U.R.
Meaning Peace, Love, Unity, Respect, this is a guiding principle in the Raver community.

Recreational drug use
MDMA (ecstasy) is associated with Raver subculture. The substance is believed to enhance sensory experiences and social bonding at raves. This belief has generated controversy, leading to legal challenges and negative stereotypes.

Trading kandi
Kandi, or colorful plastic beaded jewelry, is often exchanged at raves as a symbol of friendship.

Hair & make-up
Make-up often features glitter and bright colors. Eye make-up is typically dramatic, with heavy eyeliner and vibrant eye shadow. Hairstyles include bright colors, multiple buns or ponytails, and extensions in loud hues.

Gabbers

Originating in the Netherlands in the early 1990s, Gabber subculture centered around a fast, aggressive style of electronic dance music of the same name. The name comes from a Dutch slang term meaning "friend."

Dutch dancehall
Gabber music, which originated in Rotterdam, developed as a response to the commercialization of other electronic music scenes. It offered a harder, faster alternative to house and techno, and was embraced by working-class youth seeking a distinct identity. The rough, distorted sounds and fast tempos matched the rebellious attitude of suburban Dutch kids, shaping an identity around the music and an aggressive, in-your-face attitude.

Dress code
The Gabber look reflects the raw, unpretentious ethos and is characterized by a unisex, ultra-athletic vibe. It typically features brightly colored tracksuits, bomber jackets and comfortable clothing that allows for high-energy dancing.

Oakley Eye Jacket sunglasses

Bomber jacket

Chain necklace

Sports bra

Loose-fit jeans

Nike Air Max 90s

Hakken dance
This fast-paced dance style involves rapid footwork, jumping and stomping synchronized with the music's pounding beat, which is reminiscent of traditional European folk music.

Tecktonik

Tecktonik is a vibrant and energetic subculture.
It emerged from the French electronic
dance music scene, captivating followers
with its distinctive style, which blends Hip-Hop
and electro moves with bold fashions.

Parisian electro

Tecktonik originated in the early
2000s, primarily in the Parisian
suburbs, where underground
parties laid the foundation for
the subculture. Cyril Blanc and
Alexandre Barouzdin, two electro
dancers, significantly influenced
its development by launching
Tecktonik Killer club nights at Paris
nightclub Metropolis. The unique
dance style blends Hip-Hop,
breakdancing, waacking and
techno moves. The subculture
gained global recognition
through social media, inspiring
countless enthusiasts.

Dress code

This urban style features neon
colors, slim-fitting clothing and
bold graphic prints. Popular
items include skinny jeans, tight
T-shirts, gelled fauxhawks, and
accessories such as arm warmers
and brightly colored sneakers.

Star
face paint

Tight
T-shirt

Fingerless
gloves

Tank top

Tattoo

Neon-
colored
belt

Arm
warmers

Skinny
jeans/pants

High-top
sneakers

Metropolis
This nightclub, in Paris'
18th arrondissement,
is widely regarded as the
temple of Tecktonik.

Reality TV

Web 2.0—Interactive and user-generated content

Dot-Com Era

Marked by new-millennium optimism, the 2000s brought a playful, experimental shift in fashion and subculture. The rise of the internet democratized fashion, facilitating the exchange of styles and trends, and making them instantly accessible via online platforms and social media. The result was a truly global fashion culture.

Fashion bloggers

Britney Spears,
"Oops!... I Did It Again" (2000)

Y2K

Named after the year 2000, Y2K style emerged as a futuristic and bold aesthetic at the turn of the millennium. It captured the excitement and anxiety of the era, reflecting society's fascination with technology and new beginnings.

Millennium chic

Y2K fashion was born from the desire to embrace the digital age and widespread hopes for a bright, technologically advanced future. The style was influenced by icons like Britney Spears and Christina Aguilera, who adopted science-fiction and pop-culture influences. Metallic fabrics, holographic details, and daring separates became hallmarks of the era. As the new millennium approached, the fashion industry capitalized on the global anticipation, marketing Y2K style as a modern, playful look that embodied the spirit of the 21st century.

Dress code

Y2K style was daring, kitschy and unapologetic. It was characterized by a futuristic vibe, often combining tight-fitting, revealing cuts with bright colors and rhinestones.

❶ Baby tee
These small, tight crewneck tees often featured bold graphics, logos or catchy phrases.

❷ Juicy Couture velour tracksuit
These expensive velour tracksuits, with the word "Juicy" emblazoned on the butt, were popularized by Paris Hilton and Britney Spears, and represented the rise of athleisure and celebrity influences on fashion.

Belly-button ring

Hoop earrings

Tinted sunglasses

Bling jewelry

Platform mules

Tiny designer purse

❸

❹

Cargo pants

❺

❻

❼

Bedazzled flip phone

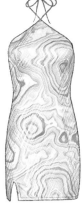

Halter-neck mini dress

Statement belt

Butterfly hair claws

❸ Low-rise jeans
Low-waist designs often revealed the wearer's underpants.

❹ Crop top
Tops that exposed the midriff were often worn with low-rise jeans or mini skirts. The sexy, abs-baring look was popularized by pop stars like Britney Spears.

❺ Von Dutch trucker hats
This brand of trucker hats kick-started a pop-culture phenomenon and epitomized the popularity of flashy logos.

❻ Micro mini skirt
These ultra-short skirts fell below the hips; sometimes belted, they often featured ruffles and pleats.

❼ Platform sneakers
With their chunky soles and heightened elevation, platform sneakers by brands like Buffalo were ubiquitous.

Logomania
From designer labels Louis Vuitton and Fendi to streetwear brands Juicy Couture and Von Dutch, logos were as important—and as large—as the products they adorned.

Paris Hilton
The OG influencer, socialite and reality-TV star was famous for her lavish lifestyle and fashion sense, which legions of fans tried to emulate. She popularized the velour tracksuit, designer bags, and other Y2K style staples.

Shine & gloss
Y2K make-up aimed to create a high-tech, futuristic look with a vibrant, shiny and radiant aesthetic. It was characterized by metallic eye shadow, lots of glitter, ultra-glossy lips, and frosted highlighter on brows and cheekbones.

Spice World (1998)

Emo

Emo, short for "emotional," emerged from the Punk-rock scene and has evolved into a multifaceted phenomenon characterized by fashion, music and attitudes.

Turning pain into a persona

Emo subculture began as an offshoot of the hardcore Punk movement in Washington, D.C., but sought to break away from that scene's aggressive and confrontational nature. Emo kids embraced introspective and emotionally charged lyrics, exploring themes such as vulnerability, relationships and personal struggles. This new style of music, which focused on expressing raw, often angst-ridden emotions, was closely tied to a dark and brooding aesthetic, which found expression in fashion, hairstyles and body modifications.

Dress code

Black is the predominant color, symbolizing emotional angst. Dark clothing, band T-shirts, skinny jeans, and accessories like studded belts, wristbands and chokers are paired with jet-black hair and long bangs.

❶ Hoodie
Often black or in a dark color, oversized hoodies are a casual and comfortable option that complements the subculture's introspective aesthetic.

❷ Piercing
Emo culture embraces body modifications, including piercings, as a form of rebellion. Facial and ear piercings like lip rings, septum piercings and ear stretchers are also seen as a way to express individuality and personal style.

❸ Skinny jeans
Originating in Punk and alternative fashions, skinny jeans are an Emo staple, typically worn tight-fitting, with a low rise, in dark colors—and often ripped.

Beanie

Fishnet stockings

Concert wristband

Low-waisted shorts

❹ Studded belt
Influenced by Punk, Emo fans also wear studded belts, sometimes with body chains hanging down from the side of the hip.

❺ Fingerless gloves/arm warmers
Punk- and Goth-influenced, arm warmers or fingerless gloves are usually made from black or dark-colored yarn or fishnet, and add an edgy vibe.

❻ Converse sneakers/Vans
Converse sneakers, especially black high-tops, and Vans skate shoes, particularly the "Authentic" or "Old Skool" styles, are popular due to their connection with alternative and skateboarding subcultures.

❼ Band T-shirt
Slim-fitting T-shirts featuring band logos or album artwork showcase Emo fans' connection to their music.

❽ Dark jewelry
Punk- and Goth-inspired jewelry, typically made from metal and leather, features dark motifs such as skulls or black hearts.

Poetry
Some Emo kids struggle with isolation and loneliness. Writing poetry can be a way to process these emotions and connect with others who may be going through similar experiences, and find a sense of community.

My Chemical Romance, *The Black Parade* (2006)

Emo ink
Tattoos often feature personal symbols, band-related imagery, and dark or sentimental themes, reflecting emotional depth and introspection.

LOVE HURTS

Hair & make-up
Hair is often styled with long, side-swept bangs and asymmetrical cuts, usually dyed dark or jet black. Make-up is characterized by heavy black eyeliner and mascara, creating a smudged look.

Scene Kids

Emerging in the early 2000s, this subculture takes its name from the local music scenes the kids frequent. Known for their vibrant fashion and love of alternative music, they are often seen as a colorful offshoot of Emo culture.

The happier Emo offspring

Scene Kid subculture developed as an offshoot of Emo. Disillusioned with the increasing negativity of Emo, Scene Kids crave a more upbeat alternative focused on self-expression, fashion and music. The subculture grew as social-media platforms like MySpace gained prominence, allowing them to connect, share fashion inspiration and promote their favorite music. The subculture's popularity peaked in the late 2000s, but remains influential in alternative fashion and music.

Dress code

Scene Kid fashion is characterized by bright clothing, often accessorized with colorful stripes, polka dots and bows. Key elements include skinny jeans, band T-shirts, platform shoes, and playful pieces such as tutus and cartoonish accessories.

❶ Tutu skirt
Inspired by Japanese Harajuku fashion, these voluminous skirts, featuring layers of tulle, add a playful, feminine touch to outfits and are often paired with leggings or fishnet tights.

❷ Striped socks
These are sometimes worn in mismatched color combinations.

Body piercing

Striped arm warmers

Choker

Mesh tights

Skinny jeans

Colored laces

Fishnet
fingerless gloves

Giant hair bow

Checkerboard stud belt

Invader Zim backpack

❸ Raccoon tail
High-contrast horizontal highlights
can be achieved with dye and bleach
or clip-on extensions.

❹ Manic Panic hair dye
Manic Panic is the go-to brand for
loud, vibrant colors.

❺ Colorful plastic jewelry
Oversized rings, rubber bracelets,
kandi and spiked cuffs add a whimsical
touch to the look. Bracelets are
sometimes worn all the way up the arm.

❻ Personalized Converse sneakers
Classic Converse sneakers are
customized with doodles, band logos
or song lyrics, making them a canvas
for self-expression.

❼ Sidekick phone
This popular phone model, released
in the early 2000s, had a QWERTY
keyboard, which was convenient for
instant messaging.

❽ Cartoon tunic tee
These long, tight-fitting T-shirts
feature cute graphics or cartoon
characters, such as GIR from *Invader
Zim* or Hello Kitty.

Profile picture taken
with MySpace angle

MySpace angle
MySpace selfies were
often taken by holding
the camera above one's
head or at an angle,
at arm's length; this
created the appearance
of a slimmer jawline
and neck.

Social-media pioneer
MySpace was a hub for Scene
Kids—they used customizable
profiles, flashy layouts and
emotive music to express
their style. Famous Scene Kids,
such as Jeffree Star, gained
substantial followings through
the platform, solidifying its
cultural significance.

RAWR XD
"Rawr" means "roar"—
the sound of a roaring
animal; XD, turned
sideways, looks like
a laughing face. RAWR
XD is a greeting,
sign-off, or expression
of excitement.

East meets West
Scene Kids are often
influenced by Japanese
fashion and pop
culture, from Harajuku
fashion's bold colors
and unique styling to
anime and J-Pop music.

Boho Chic

The fusion of bohemianism and fashion reflected a relaxed, free-spirited and artistic style. Its name originates from the lifestyle associated with counterculture movements and artists.

Middle-class modern hippies
Boho Chic emerged in the early 2000s, influenced by the aesthetics of the 1960s and 1970s Hippie movement, but with a modern, sophisticated twist. Celebrities including Sienna Miller, Kate Moss and the Olsen sisters popularized the look, which quickly gained traction in the fashion industry. The appeal of Boho Chic lies in its nonconformist approach to fashion, allowing individuals to express themselves through eclectic, vintage-inspired and layered ensembles that defy traditional fashion rules and emphasize creativity.

Dress code
Boho Chic embraces flowy, natural fabrics, and features elements like lace, fringe and embroidery. Earth tones dominate the color palette, complemented by vibrant patterns. Accessories include layered necklaces, oversized sunglasses and wide-brimmed hats, with an emphasis on vintage, handmade and unique pieces.

Tribal-inspired jewelry

Large belt

Denim shorts

Wide-brimmed hat

Cowboy boots

Glastonbury Festival
This annual contemporary performing arts festival in Somerset, England, features music, comedy, theatre, dance and other art forms.

Twee

The Twee aesthetic is characterized by a nostalgic, vintage-inspired charm and whimsical, innocent nature. "Twee" is a British word that means overly sweet or precious.

Uncool is the new cool

Twee style took off on Tumblr in the early 2000s as a reaction to mainstream commercial fashion. It was popularized by indie artists and Twee-pop musicians who embraced a more authentic aesthetic. The movement was heavily influenced by vintage styles such as 1960s Mod culture and mid-century Americana. Twee style was a celebration of individuality and simplicity; adherents embraced imperfection, childishness and quirkiness.

Dress code

Twee style favors vintage or vintage-inspired clothing such as Peter Pan collars, cardigans and A-line dresses. Gingham, plaid, polka dots and florals are prevalent. Accessories include oversized glasses and brooches, often featuring animals or other whimsical elements.

Cardigan

Thick-framed glasses

Peter Pan collar

Polka dots

Black tights

Flared dress

Ballet flats

Belle & Sebastian, *The Boy with the Arab Strap* (1996)

Twee pop

This subgenre of indie music is characterized by whimsical lyrics, light and airy melodies, and jangly guitars. Twee pop revolves around innocent and nostalgic themes, and celebrates the simple pleasures of life—love, friendship and everyday experiences.

MK Boys & Girls

MK is an abbreviation of Mongkok, a bustling district of Hong Kong where young people gather and shop, embracing their unconventional fashion and lifestyle.

Cheap chic in the concrete jungle

The MK Boy and Girl subculture emerged in the late 1990s and early 2000s as a means of self-expression and identity amidst the fast-paced development of Hong Kong. Mongkok, a crowded commercial area with low-cost shopping and dining options, became a social center for working-class young people. The subculture draws inspiration from various global influences, including Japanese street fashion, Taiwanese pop icons, and Western Punk, and blends them into a local style that reflects Hong Kong's cultural diversity.

Dress code

MK Boys and Girls are known for their eclectic fashion sense and street-style looks. Key elements include dyed hair, ripped jeans for boys and Japanese-influenced *kawaii* styles for girls.

Black tank top/T-shirt

Long bangs

Kawaii-style top

Hot pants

Ripped jeans

Flip-flops

Karaoke

MK Boys and Girls often gather in karaoke bars, where they enjoy singing Cantopop songs and socializing with their friends.

Shamate

This Chinese subculture emerged in the early 2000s. The name *Shamate* (杀马特) is a Chinese transliteration of the word for "smart." Shamate is characterized by outlandish fashions and hairstyles that challenge conventions.

A community for the uprooted
Shamate subculture originated among working-class migrant youths seeking a sense of identity and belonging in a rapidly urbanizing China. As these young people moved from rural areas to urban centers for work, mostly in factories, they found solace in the Shamate community, which provided a means of self-expression and connection. The subculture often unintentionally draws inspiration from various global influences, particularly Japanese Visual Kei and Western Goth and Emo styles.

Dress code
Characterized by unconventional aesthetics, Shamate style combines elements of Punk, Goth, and Visual Kei. Key elements include outrageous hairstyles and clothing inspired by foreign bands, fashion trends and pop-culture icons.

***We Were Smart* (2019)**
This documentary by Chinese filmmaker Li Yifan explores the lives of Shamate. The film delves into their experiences, motivations and struggles while addressing broader social issues such as urbanization, income inequality and globalization.

Long, exaggerated hairstyles
Frequently styled in dramatic shapes, Shamate hairdos were often sprayed bright colors that could be washed out; that way they could go back to their normal hairstyle the next day for work.

Seapunk

Seapunk subculture, which emerged in the early
2010s, combines aquatic themes with Punk
and Cyber aesthetics. The name reflects its oceanic
inspiration and the Punk attitude that underlies
its ethos.

Aquatic internet fantasy

Seapunk emerged in 2011 as
an online microculture. Originating
on Tumblr and Twitter, it revolved
around a tongue-in-cheek
fascination with all things nautical.
The heavily filtered and distorted
aquatic imagery evoked an
ironic and exaggerated version
of mid-'90s internet aesthetics.
As Seapunk gained traction, it
evolved into a broader subculture
that encompassed music, fashion
and art. Its unique visual style
often incorporated oceanic
motifs, vivid colors and digital
imagery, lending a surreal and
whimsical atmosphere.

Dress code

Seapunk embraces aquatic
themes and vibrant colors,
with an emphasis on blues and
greens. Key elements include
holographic and iridescent
materials, ocean-inspired prints,
and Cyberpunk-influenced
accessories. Clothing often
features marine life, geometric
patterns and digital graphics.

❶ Retro internet graphic prints
Prints with early computer-generated
imagery feature aquatic elements
inspired by the '90s internet and the
intersection of nature and technology.

❷ Face gems
Sparkling rhinestone stickers are
often applied on the forehead, around
the eyes or on cheeks.

Glitter
elements

Blue/green
lipstick

Tie-dye
T-shirt

Platform
shoes

Shell-shaped accessories

Round sunglasses

Translucent backpack

Tight mesh top

Iridescent choker

Jelly shoes

❸ Yin-yang motif
The yin and yang symbol depicts balance between opposing forces—such as nature and technology—reflecting Seapunk's fusion of aquatic themes and cyber aesthetics.

❹ Fishnet elements
Fishnet tights, tops and gloves are popular due to their association with Punk and Goth styles, as well as their visual connection to fishing nets and the ocean.

❻ Holographic elements
Holographic materials mimic the shimmer of water. Clothing such as jackets, leggings and skirts with iridescent finishes are popular for their eye-catching and futuristic appearance.

❺ Transparent raincoat
Transparent clothing, including raincoats made of PVC or plastic, have a water-like appearance that connects to the aquatic theme.

❼ Ocean-themed jewelry
Fun, colorful plastic jewelry features ocean themes including dolphins, shells, starfish and seahorses.

Lil Internet's Seapunk origin tweet (June 1, 2011)

Born on Twitter
A Twitter exchange between two multimedia producers—@lilinternet and @lilgovernment—immortalized Seapunk culture via #SEAPUNK.

Unicorn Kid, *Tidal Rave* (2011)

Seapunk music
This blend of electronic dance beats with aquatic sounds draws inspiration from '90s rave, ambient and Hip-Hop. It has influenced other music styles, including vaporwave and future funk, while remaining a niche genre.

Azealia Banks, *Atlantis* (2012)

Web1.0 Graphics
Characterized by '90s internet-inspired, retro-futuristic oceanic themes, Seapunk digital art was popularized on Tumblr, where users can create and discover related posts, images, music and videos via the tagging system.

Hipsters

The term "Hipster" was first coined in the 1940s to describe jazz enthusiasts who rejected mainstream culture. "Hip" means in the know about the latest music, cultural trends and new ideas.

The quest for authentic living

During the early 2000s, Hipster subculture began to emerge in urban areas like Brooklyn, New York. Driven by a desire for uniqueness and authenticity, its adherents sought escape from mainstream consumerism. This manifested in a rediscovery of vintage or old-timey fashions, music, crafts and foods. A fondness for "the old ways" was considered a statement against homogenization, a celebration of individuality, and nostalgia for a bygone era. Hipsters were usually associated with progressive political ideologies and an appreciation of art, creativity and intellectual pursuits.

Dress code

The Hipster look was stylish but not overly trendy. Characterized by vintage finds and an eclectic mix of styles, with elements such as artisanal leather goods, vintage T-shirts, and tote bags that reflect their ideologies, the emphasis was on individuality and nonconformity.

❶ Beard
From the full beard to the carefully groomed goatee, facial hair is synonymous with the Hipster image. It is a sign of rugged masculinity and a nod to a time when beards and mustaches were more prevalent.

❷ Tattoos
Hipster tattoos often feature hand-drawn designs, including geometric patterns, vintage illustrations and symbols.

Vintage half-rim glasses

Vintage jacket

Bow tie

Rolled-up jeans

Cut-off jeans

iPhone

Converse sneakers

Skinny jeans

Plaid flannel shirt

Wide-brimmed fedora

Beanie

NO THANK YOU

Scarf

Band T-shirt

❸ Leather boots
Popular among both men and women, often in distressed or vintage leather.

❹ Plaid flannel shirt
These were often worn loosely or buttoned up to the neck, and were a key element of the hipster aesthetic due to their comfortable, vintage appeal.

❺ Tote bag
Tote bags served as canvases for personal expression. Their popularity aligned with the hipster ethos of sustainability and conscious consumption.

❻ Messenger bag/satchel
Often made from leather, Hipsters' bags exude a vintage, scholarly vibe.

❼ Thick-framed glasses
Chunky spectacles, often in a Wayfarer or round style, exuded intellectual chic and were a trademark of the Hipster aesthetic.

❽ Fixed-gear bicycle
"Fixies" were admired for their simplicity and efficiency. The single-speed design, lack of brakes, and direct pedal-to-wheel connection made them the minimalist's choice.

Vintage values
Hipsters redefined modernity with a nostalgic twist—vinyl records, 35mm film cameras and vintage clothing were considered cherished items that encapsulated the timeless essence of aesthetics and functionality.

A return to craftsmanship
Hipsters appreciated craftsmanship and found solace in the tangible authenticity of craft beers, artisanal coffee and handmade products. This revival of traditional skills signified a deep-rooted love of quality over quantity.

Barber shop revival
Barber shops were rediscovered as sanctuaries of masculinity. The art of grooming merged with a vintage aesthetic, making every haircut and shave an experience steeped in heritage and craftsmanship.

Instagram
The platform served as a digital canvas for Hipster subculture, showcasing their artisanal lifestyle, vintage finds and sustainable initiatives.

Hypebeasts

The term "Hypebeast" comes from the fusion of "hype," denoting a trend's popularity, and "beast," referring to the relentless pursuit of such trends. This subculture revolves around high-end streetwear, music and the thirst for the latest, most sought-after goods.

Rare kicks and hype culture

The Hypebeast subculture started to crystallize in the late '90s and early 2000s in New York City, initially as a small group of enthusiasts passionate about collecting rare sneakers and streetwear. Its popularity surged with the rise of Hip-Hop culture and the skateboard scene; style icons including Pharrell Williams and Kanye West embraced and promoted the lifestyle. Leading streetwear brands like Supreme, Stüssy, and A Bathing Ape (BAPE) became synonymous with Hypebeast style, which soon become a global phenomenon.

Dress code

Hypebeasts are considered both stylish and trendy, combining high-end designer labels with streetwear brands. Key pieces include limited-edition sneakers, graphic T-shirts, oversized outerwear, and accessories such as backpacks and caps, often featuring bold logos and unconventional designs.

❶ Logomania
Bold logos and monograms showcase status, exclusivity, wealth and niche fashion knowledge.

❷ Oversized branded T-shirt
Typically from high-end streetwear brands such as Off-White and BAPE, extra-large tees usually feature big graphics and logos.

Nike Air Jordan sneakers

Skate shorts

Limited-edition sneakers

Logo belt

Supreme backpack

New Era cap

Nike SB Dunk sneakers

Branded sweatpants

③ Evisu jeans
Popularized by Hip-Hop artists including Jay-Z, Evisu jeans' hand-painted designs and traditional Japanese denim techniques set them apart.

④ BAPE Shark hoodie
Designed by Nigo, the founder of A Bathing Ape, the hoodie features a cartoon shark face and camo body. It is now a streetwear icon.

⑤ Louis Vuitton duffel bag
The classic LV duffel features the monogram or Damier pattern. Crossover editions with Supreme and Takashi Murakami are hugely sought after.

⑥ Stüssy T-shirt
Stüssy is of the original streetwear brands, and its graphic T-shirts were a must-have item in the 2000s.

⑦ Supreme box logo hoodie
Also known as the BOGO hoodie, the design and scarcity of this product has made it a must-have for Hypebeasts.

The riot shoe
The 2005 release of the Nike SB Dunk Low Pigeon was a defining moment in Hypebeast culture. The limited-edition sneaker caused a frenzy outside Reed Space in New York; the *New York Post* featured the melee on its front page, bringing the phenomenon to mainstream attention.

Supreme
Originally a skate shop in New York, Supreme played a key role in popularizing the limited-edition-drop model, a hallmark of Hypebeast culture. Supreme's exclusive releases, often selling out in seconds, have created a cult following.

Pharrell Williams
Williams was key figure in shaping the Hypebeast aesthetic, blending streetwear with luxury. His label, Billionaire Boys Club, and collaborations with luxury brands including Chanel, embody this genre-defying approach.

Baddies

The Baddie subculture came from social media, especially Instagram. It refers to those who call themselves "bad girls"—edgy, confident women who embrace their sexuality.

Insta style: a redefinition of beauty

Baddie style started in the early 2010s with influencers showcasing their unapologetic, glamorous lifestyles and fashion-forward looks on Instagram. The moniker refers to their fearless approach to trends and self-expression. The rise of the Baddies was fueled by a shift toward body positivity and self-love, which resonated with many young people. The style, popularized by celebrities including Cardi B and Kim Kardashian, offered an alternative to traditional beauty standards, promoting a more diverse and inclusive definition of attractiveness.

Dress code

Staples of Baddie style include high-end streetwear, body-hugging outfits and branded accessories. The style is often revealing, with a focus on showcasing one's best features. Heels, crop tops, ripped jeans and luxury handbags are must-haves.

❶ Bodycon jumpsuit
A stretchy, form-fitting full-body jumpsuit highlights the figure; it was popularized by Kim Kardashian and other celebrities.

❷ Acrylic nails
Long, embellished acrylic or gel nails are typical for Baddies. Rhinestones, airbrushing and unique shapes take nails to the next level.

Hoop earrings

Bra top

PVC sandals

Statement jewelry

Designer bag

Bodycon dress

Cut-out bodysuit

Faux-leather leggings

Lace-up heels

Oversized sunglasses

❸ Tracksuit
These coordinated sets add a level of sophistication to the otherwise casual streetwear-inspired look, paired with sneakers for a daytime look or heels for an evening out.

❹ Ripped jeans
Often high-waisted, jeans elongate the legs and emphasize curves; distressed or ripped details add edginess.

❺ Crop top
Crop tops that accentuate the waistline range from simple athletic styles to off-shoulder versions and those with cut-outs or strings.

❻ Chunky sneakers
Also known as "dad shoes," chunky sneakers add a street-style feel and are favored for their comfort and statement-making capacity.

❼ Oversized sunglasses
Oversized sunnies add an element of mystery and glamour. Designer styles make a statement and are seen as a status symbol.

Sculpting surgery
Baddies regularly opt for plastic surgery—butt lifts, lip fillers and the like—to achieve what is often considered an unrealistic body ideal, influenced by societal pressures and the desire for perfection.

Instagram is life
For Baddies, Instagram is more than a platform—it's a lifestyle. It's where they showcase their daring outfits, flawless make-up and enviable lifestyles. Through carefully curated photos and content, they build their personal brand, cultivating a following that admires their aesthetic and attitude.

Contour & highlight
These techniques define and enhance facial features, creating a sculpted and polished look. The art of shadow and light complements Baddies' bold, confident style.

Afropunks

Afropunk is a vibrant subculture of African-American fans of Punk. The name stems from a 2003 documentary of the same name, which highlighted Black participation in what had been a predominantly white subculture.

Black Punk rebels

Afropunk was a response to the underrepresentation and marginalization of African-Americans in the Punk scene. Many African-Americans felt unwelcome and out of place in mainstream Punk circles, so they formed their own community, which blended Punk ideologies with Black culture and activism. The annual Afropunk Festival, which started in 2005, has become a global event celebrating culture, music, art and fashion while promoting inclusivity and diversity.

Dress code

Afropunk fashion is an eclectic mix of Punk elements, African-inspired patterns, vibrant colors and streetwear. Bold accessories, body art and unconventional hairstyles are common, making the aesthetic a spectacular display of individuality, creativity and cultural pride.

Body jewelry

Hairstyles may include locs, braids, afros or twists.

Tribal-inspired accessories

Black skinny jeans

African-inspired prints

Afro-Punk (2003), a documentary by James Spooner

Renegades

Renegades are Black heavy-metal fans in Botswana. The name reflects their rebellious spirit and love of the powerful soundscapes of heavy metal, while infusing their own cultural identity and style into the mix.

Heavy-metal mavericks
Botswana's heavy-metal culture emerged in the late 1970s. The music resonated with those seeking a means of self-expression, leading to the creation of this unique subculture. Renegade attire combines Western cowboy and biker aesthetics with African elements, and symbolizes rebellion and individuality. Inspired by both local and international heavy metal bands, Renegades have created a scene that celebrates freedom, strength and a deep love of music.

Dress code
Renegades typically don leather outfits, cowboy boots and bandannas, a style reminiscent of biker gangs and Western cowboys. Some personalize their outfits with African prints, motifs or accessories, creating a unique fusion of global metal fashion with local cultural pride.

Crackdust, *Dented Reality* (2006)

Botswana bands Overthrust, Crackdust and Wrust play death metal, which they sometimes mix with African musical traditions and imagery.

Leather cowboy hat

Leather biker jacket

Band T-shirt

Skull belt buckle

Body chains and metal trinkets

Studs

Black chaps

Cowboy boots

Normcore

Normcore is an anti-fashion aesthetic that embraces the ordinary. It's an antidote to the need for novelty and extravagance, advocating simplicity, comfort and "uncool" everyday attire.

Ordinary is the new black
A reaction to fashion's constant push for new trends, Normcore was first identified by trend forecasting agency K-Hole, which described it as a desire to be "blank" in response to the saturation of uniqueness in the digital age. Normcore rejects the idea of emphasizing individuality and signaling one's status through style, and suggests an alternative: a low-key, understated aesthetic that does not stand out. Normcore embraces the idea of dressing like everyone else as an act of liberation.

Dress code
Normcore is all about inconspicuousness, simplicity and utilitarianism. Basic and unbranded clothing like plain T-shirts, jeans, sweatpants, sneakers and hoodies can be mixed and matched for an understated look.

❶ Shirt jacket
A shirt jacket is also known as a "shacket." Often made from bulkier fabric than a shirt, it can be worn as a light jacket or layered under a coat.

❷ Straight-fit jeans
Comfortable and versatile, high-waisted jeans with a relaxed fit were a reaction against the tight, low-rise jeans of the early 2000s.

❸ Birkenstocks
Appreciated for their anti-fashion, crunchy appeal, Birkenstocks are known for their cork soles, leather straps, comfortable design and durability.

Crewneck sweater

Beanie

Chinos

Joggers/
track pants

Basic hoodie/
sweatshirt

Basic sneakers

Raw denim jeans

Boxy button-down shirt

④ Unstructured blazer
Often paired with a T-shirt, jeans
and sneakers, an unlined or half-lined
blazer made from soft fabric, with a
loose fit, adds a bit of formality
without compromising on comfort.

⑤ Fleece jacket/ pullover
Often in solid colors, this comfortable
and practical staple—and its somewhat
dated look—fit the Normcore
preference for non-trendy clothes.

⑥ Plain T-shirt
A Normcore wardrobe isn't complete
without high-quality, solid-color
T-shirts; nothing beats
the combination of well-made, versatile
and comfortable.

⑦ Baseball cap
Plain baseball caps, sometimes with
understated logos, are inspired by
stereotypical suburban-dad attire.

⑧ New Balance sneakers
New Balance are known for their
comfort and durability, and
their chunky, "unfashionable"
design—especially the 992 model—
fits perfectly with Normcore.

"Normcore isn't about rebelling against or giving
into the status quo, it's about letting go of the need to
look distinctive, to make time for something new."

—Fiona Duncan, *New York* magazine

Nordic aesthetics
Simplicity and functionality
are core tenets of Nordic
design. With a focus
on high-quality materials,
muted color palettes
and pieces that defy
trends, Nordic brands
including Norse Projects
and Arket represent the
Normcore preference
for understated, durable
and versatile clothing.

Steve Jobs
Jobs' daily uniform—black
turtleneck, Levi's 501s, and New
Balance 992s—was not just
a fashion statement but
a strategic decision to reduce
decision fatigue. His style
symbolized the ideals of comfort,
simplicity, and the rejection of
fashion's fickleness.

Common Projects
New York brand Common
Projects is known for its minimalist
sneakers, quality materials
and craftsmanship. The absence
of visible logos resonates
with Normcore's preference for
unpretentious, high-quality,
versatile items.

K-Pop

Originating in South Korea, K-Pop is not only a global musical craze but a blend of pop music, fashion and cultural expression.

East-meets-all phenomenon
K-Pop fashion emerged alongside South Korea's booming pop music industry in the late '90s and early 2000s. Rooted in the country's vibrant and dynamic culture, K-Pop fashion draws inspiration from a variety of sources, including traditional Korean clothing, Western high fashion, streetwear, and even elements of Japanese and Chinese fashion. This eclectic blend reflects the energetic and diverse nature of K-Pop itself, promoting a unique style that transcends borders and resonates with fans around the world.

Dress code
Eclectic and showy, K-Pop fashion varies widely, reflecting the diversity of the musical genre. Common elements include oversized clothing, colorful patterns, layering and a mix of streetwear and high fashion.

❶ Bold suit
Often worn for performances, music videos and public appearances, a bold suit might be a single color or patterned—the point is to create a striking look and add an element of theatricality.

Traditional Korean clothing elements

Turtleneck sweater

Earring

❶

Mini skirt

Platform boots

High-waisted shorts

Bucket hat

Overcoat

Statement jewelry

Gentle Monster sunglasses

Baseball hat

❷ Wide-leg pants
A staple of both male and female K-Pop wardrobes, wide-leg pants are often worn with fitted tops to create a balanced silhouette.

❸ High-waisted jeans
High-waisted designs elongate the legs. Often paired with crop tops or tucked-in shirts, they are worn as part of casual, everyday outfits or can be dressed up for performances and public appearances.

❹ Oversized shirt
Loose and baggy, oversized shirts' popularity can be traced back to streetwear.

❺ Canada Goose parka
K-Pop groups started wearing the parkas as part of their "airport fashion" looks; this helped turn Canada Goose into a luxury fashion megabrand.

❻ White platform sneakers
These add height and elongate the legs, as well as giving off an edgy, youthful vibe and adding drama.

❼ Tight crop top
Often worn by female K-Pop stars, crop tops show off toned figures. They are a symbol of the confidence and boldness that K-Pop stars embody.

Airport fashion
Fans emulate the stylish travel attire of K-Pop idols by wearing a mix of comfortable staples and high-fashion pieces: oversized hoodies, bucket hats, face masks and designer bags.

Blackpink, Ice Cream (2020)

Music & fashion
Fashion in K-Pop serves a crucial role in distinguishing individual groups and their concepts. Outfits are carefully curated to align with each music project, enhancing the visual storytelling and musical experience.

Make-up for men
Male K-Pop idols popularized the make-up trend, pushing beyond traditional gender norms. The look typically features a flawless base, eyeliner and eye shadow, and is often completed with soft, gradient lips.

Flash Fashi

In the era of smartphones and social media, trends became short-lived "vibes" and microtrends emerged rapidly, no longer dictated by large brands but shaped by an interconnected online community. This shift, reflective of rapid technological progress, marked the dawn of truly participatory fashion.

TikTok (2016)

First iPhone (2007)

Netflix streaming (2007)

PARIS2015
UN CLIMATE CHANGE CONFERENCE
COP21·CMP11

The Paris Agreement (2015)

The Avengers (2012)

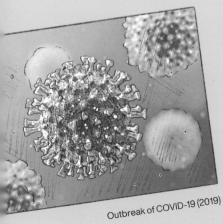

Outbreak of COVID-19 (2019)

VSCO Girls

This look got its name from the photo-editing app of the same name; its filters can create a beach-inspired, vintage look. The trend, which started among young women, is characterized by its eco-friendly lifestyle and laid-back aesthetic.

Eco-conscious So-Cal style

The VSCO subculture really took off in 2019, largely on platforms like TikTok, Instagram and YouTube. Many believe its popularity stemmed from a nostalgic longing for a simple, relaxed lifestyle, in contrast to the fast-paced digital world. The trend also reflects an eco-conscious mentality, championing sustainable brands, products and practices and resonating with young people's growing environmental concerns. The subculture embodies a sunny, carefree image, drawing inspiration from '90s fashion and Southern California beach culture.

Dress code

VSCO fashion emphasizes comfort and sustainability with a casual and colorful aesthetic. Fashion staples are oversized pastel or tie-dye T-shirts, high-waisted denim and Birkenstock sandals. Clothing is often thrifted, and reusable water bottles are ubiquitous.

❶ Oversized T-shirt
Comfy and casual, oversized tees are often in pastel colors or tie-dyed. The fit is reminiscent of '90s fashions.

❷ Birkenstocks
Originating in Germany, these sandals are popular for their comfort and durability. Their simple, earthy design aligns with the VSCO Girl aesthetic.

Vans slip-ons

Crop top

Metal straws

Starbucks iced coffee

Stickers

Crocs

Mom jeans

③ High-waisted denim shorts
Another nod to '90s fashion, denim shorts are often thrifted, supporting the subculture's emphasis on sustainable fashion.

④ Fjällräven Kånken backpack
The Swedish brand's commitment to sustainability resonates with the green credentials of VSCO Girls. The backpacks are recognized for their durability, simple design, and wide range of colors.

⑤ Instant camera
Instant cameras are popular for their vintage, nostalgic appeal, ability to create tangible memories, and decorative potential. The photos' hazy and warm tone resembles the look of the VSCO app's filters.

⑥ Hydro Flask water bottle
Often customized with stickers, these bottles are well-insulated, keeping beverages cold for extended periods. Their wide-mouth design accommodates ice cubes, making them perfect for hydrating during warm beach days.

⑦ Scrunchie
These '90s hair accessories made a comeback due to their functionality and retro appeal. They're used to tie up messy buns, or worn as bracelets.

⑧ Friendship bracelet
Handmade, colorful bracelets symbolize the community aspect of the subculture. They're often exchanged among friends.

⑨ Puka-shell jewelry
Symbolizing beach culture, these necklaces are a nod to VSCO Girls' love of the ocean and nature.

VSCO filter
An acronym for Visual Supply Company, VSCO is a photography app known for its wide array of filters. They are designed to mimic the look of classic film cameras, giving photos a vintage aesthetic.

VSCO expressions
The subculture has its own slang, with phrases like "sksksk" (a keyboard smash expressing laughter or excitement) and "and I oop," a phrase expressing surprise or embarrassment that is borrowed from internet and drag culture.

"Save the turtles"
This phrase, often used by VSCO Girls, expresses their environmental consciousness and symbolizes their advocacy for reducing plastic waste, specifically plastic straws, to protect marine life—particularly sea turtles.

Coconut Girls

This 2000s nostalgia-centric trend got its name from the tropical vibes it embodies. Coconut Girls embrace a beachy, vivid aesthetic that's reminiscent of the islands—a sun-soaked, coconut-laden paradise.

Escapism through tropical style

The trend originated in the early 2010s among young women enamored with tropical locales such as Hawaii and California. The look was a playful, nostalgic callback to the surf culture of the 1960s. In the early 2020s it rapidly gained popularity on TikTok; this may be attributed to the longing for a carefree escape—especially amid the pandemic. Inspired by early-2000s pop-culture references like the movie *Blue Crush* and music by Sheryl Crow, the Coconut Girl trend represents a retreat to simpler times.

Dress code

Coconut Girls achieve a laid-back, beachy vibe with tropical prints, hibiscus motifs and sarongs. Key staples include tie-dye, beaded accessories and slip dresses. The look is complemented with ocean-themed jewelry, flip flops or sandals, and flowers.

Temporary tattoo

Bell-bottom jeans

❶ Halter-neck top
To fit the vacation vibe, halter-necks are often made of lightweight fabric, crocheted or knitted in bright colors and tropical patterns.

❷ Sarong
Originating in Southeast Asia, sarongs are versatile pieces that can be worn as skirts, dresses or scarves.

❸ Crochet crop top
These crop tops with a bohemian vibe can be made from cotton yarn.

Tropical-print mini skirt

Sunscreen lotion

Hawaiian hibiscus print

Flower claw clip

Bikini

Floral bucket hat

❹ Platform flip-flops
Influenced by Y2K culture, platform flip-flops are an important element.

❺ Sundress
Light, breezy dresses with halter necks or thin straps are often made from tie-dye, floral or tropical-print fabric with crochet details.

❻ Shell jewelry
Necklaces, bracelets or earrings made from seashells are a nod to the ocean. They're popular for their natural, earthy aesthetic.

❼ High-waisted shorts
With a retro, '90s vibe, high-waisted shorts' flattering cut emphasizes the waist. They are often made from denim or linen.

❽ Raffia bag
Often handmade, these bags are associated with traditional craft techniques. They're popular for their sustainable aspect and the touch of rustic charm they add to outfits.

❾ Plumeria accessories
Plumeria, also known as frangipani, is a tropical flower from Hawaii. A real flower can be worn in the hair, or simply jewelry and accessories with the motif.

Tropical drink
Tropical drinks are a reflection of Coconut Girl style. Coconut water, pineapple smoothies or well-garnished piña coladas not only taste like a sun-drenched vacation, but also align visually with the beach aesthetic.

Sun-kissed skin
The look is all about a natural, radiant glow that appears as if one has spent a day in the sun. The aim is to mimic the gentle tan and rosy flush one would get at the beach.

Seaglass
Colorful, ocean-tumbled treasures, collected while beachcombing, encapsulate the aesthetic.

Aquamarine (2006)
This movie, about two teenage girls who discover a mermaid in their beach club's swimming pool, embodies Y2K aesthetics, friendships and a lighthearted, sunny vibe.

Soft Boys & Girls

Soft Boys and Girls emerged from online platforms like TikTok. The term "soft" signifies a style and demeanor that embraces gentleness, vulnerability and traditionally feminine traits, regardless of gender.

⬆ Pastel sunglasses
A popular accessory among Soft Girls, pastel sunglasses come in cute shapes and many colors.

Round wire-rimmed glasses

Fluffy hoodie

Sensitivity has no gender

Rooted in Gen Z's exploration of gender norms, "soft" styles provide an alternative to the tougher, more detached coolness associated with Skater or E-Boy and E-Girl aesthetics. Soft Boys and Soft Girls embrace emotional openness, sensitivity and a pastel-colored style, reflecting a departure from traditional gender stereotypes and a broader cultural shift toward emotional intelligence and self-care.

Cropped cardigan

Dress code

Soft Boys and Girls prefer pastels and muted colors, oversized knitwear or shirts, and high-waisted jeans. Accessories include beaded bracelets, butterfly motifs and flower crowns. The look is comfortable and non-threatening, mirroring the gentle demeanor associated with the aesthetic.

Pleated tennis dress/ mini dress

Nike Air Force 1 sneakers

Harry Styles

Styles is often cited as a Soft Boy for his embrace of androgynous fashions. He wears pastels and floral prints, and his song lyrics explore themes of emotional vulnerability and introspection.

Chunky sneakers

Sailor Moon
A typical Soft Girl figure in manga, Sailor Moon—a.k.a. Usagi Tsukino—is a schoolgirl who does not hide her feelings. She has stereotypically girly and romantic interests.

Retro bucket hat

Tie-front cardigan

Crop top/ baby tee

Oversized crewneck sweater

High-waisted mom jeans

Cute motifs, e.g. clouds, butterflies

Loose-fitting white shirt

Baguette bag

Faded jeans

Converse sneakers

➕ Hair accessories
Butterfly hair clips, large snap hair clips and scrunchies in pastel colors are important in the Soft Girl look.

➕ Dainty jewelry
Soft Girls often wear delicate jewelry with tiny butterfly, star or heart charms, and often layer the chains.

E-Boys & Girls

The E-Boy and Girl aesthetic emerged as a trend in the 2010s, primarily on TikTok; it then went viral on other social-media platforms. The "E" stands for electronic, reflecting the subculture's digital origins.

Ripped fishnet top/tights

Chunky ring

Choker

🔊 Cat-ear gaming headphones
Early E-Girls were associated with gaming and Japanese anime culture. Pastel gaming headphones with cute cat ears were a popular accessory.

Boxy, collared shirt

Joggers

🔊 Silver jewelry
Inspired by Punk and Goth, chunky silver jewelry is often worn in multiples.

Cargo pants

Lil Peep
Rapper Lil Peep's face tattoo, unique blend of Emo and Hip-Hop music, and mix of vintage clothing and streetwear made him influential in the development of E-Boy culture.

Dr. Martens boots

Edgy introverts

E-Boy and E-Girl culture began as teenage introverts shared their looks on social media. The subculture was a form of self-expression inspired by the dark and edgy aesthetic of Emo, Punk and Goth. Young people were drawn to the emotionally intense and introspective music as well as the ethos of individualism and nonconformity. The style also facilitated gender fluidity; E-Boys and E-Girls exhibited femininity inspired by K-Pop, while the make-up reflected the influence of Japanese manga and online gaming.

Dress code

E-Boy and E-Girl fashion emphasizes a K-Pop-like, androgynous mix of black and pastel colors. Extra edginess is key; layered T-shirts or crop tops, tight-fitting pants or mini skirts, bondage gear and chains are often paired with fishnets and Dr. Martens boots.

Padlock necklace

Band T-shirt

Striped long-sleeved T-shirt

Belt chain

Tight black jeans

Plaid skirt

White tube socks

Face art
E-Girls often paint hearts or other motifs under their eyes, apply heavy blush on cheeks and nose, and add fake freckles on top.

O-face
Also known as *ahegao* face (アヘ顔), this expression originated in Japanese *hentai* (adult anime) manga. It has since become popular in some online communities as a form of self-expression and humor.

Art Hoes

Art Hoe was started by two Tumblr users, Mars and Jam, who wanted to reclaim derogatory language and create a space for Black women in the art world. It has since grown into a thriving subculture.

Beret

Round, wire-rimmed glasses

Challenging art-world norms

The Art Hoe movement started in 2015 as a reaction to stereotyping and a lack of representation of people of color, especially Black women, in the art world. Through social media platforms like Tumblr and Instagram, Mars and Jam challenged those norms by encouraging individuals to share their artistic expressions and interpretations. The movement quickly gained traction on these platforms, where people began to identify with and contribute to the Art Hoe aesthetic and philosophy, spreading its influence globally.

Fjällräven Kånken backpack

Turtleneck sweater

Mom jeans

Meadow stripes

Dress code

Art Hoes often wear a unique and eclectic mix of vintage and contemporary fashion. Key elements include mustard yellow, colorful patterned clothing, round glasses and items featuring the works of famous artists, symbolizing a direct connection to art.

Dr. Martens boots

Art prints
The works of Vincent Van Gogh, Jean-Michel Basquiat and Yayoi Kusama are often featured on Art Hoe clothing and accessories.

Converse sneakers

Plant Parents

Plant Parents are a growing subculture that centers around indoor gardening, especially among millennials; it involves nurturing houseplants, symbolizing a shift toward a more sustainable and nature-connected lifestyle in the confines of urban living.

Greenery soothes urban souls

The movement was fueled by an increasing awareness of climate change and the benefits of greenery. Urbanization and digital saturation led many to seek respite in nature, and houseplants offered an accessible solution. Social media platforms such as Instagram and Pinterest became a hub for sharing plant-care tips and showcasing indoor jungles, propelling the trend's popularity. The movement represents a desire to cultivate life and embrace a slow, mindful way of living.

Dress code

Plant Parents typically wear comfortable gear that allows them to move around easily. Clothing is often in nature-inspired patterns and earth tones, and accessories are made from natural materials like linen, cotton and bamboo.

Plant whisperer

With a deep sense of what plants need, Plant Parents view plant care as a dialogue, fostering a deep symbiotic relationship. Some will talk to their plants, because they believe that plants respond positively to human voices.

Loose T-shirt

Wool sweater

Denim overalls

Mom jeans

Vans/Converse sneakers

Dark Academia

This subculture emerged on online platforms, primarily Tumblr. It got its name due to its emphasis on classic literature, the pursuit of self-discovery, and an aesthetic inspired by academia and the Gothic period.

Modern Gothic collegiate
Dark Academia romanticizes the world of elite universities, particularly their aesthetic and their intellectual rigor. The subculture embodies a deep nostalgia for classic literature, philosophy and the hallowed halls of old libraries. The "dark" in Dark Academia is influenced by Gothic and classic literature, including Mary Shelley's *Frankenstein* and the novels of Fyodor Dostoevsky. These texts explore the darker aspects of human nature, adding a layer of mystique to the academic ideal.

Dress code
Dark Academia leans heavily into a preppy, scholarly aesthetic. Key elements include tweed blazers, turtlenecks, vintage glasses, dark pants and pleated skirts, predominantly in a color palette of black and earth tones.

Hair ribbon

Leather belt

Tweed blazer

V-neck sweater

Turtleneck sweater

Trench coat

Classic dark plaid

Ankle boots

Vintage watch

Dress pants

Oxford shoes

The Picture of Dorian Gray (1891)
This Gothic novel by Oscar Wilde is a tale of corruption and decadence. It follows the transformation of a young man who sells his soul for eternal youth and beauty.

Light Academia

This counterpart to Dark Academia reflects a more optimistic aesthetic and ethos: a love of learning entwined with an appreciation for the beauty and light in everyday life.

Bright & hopeful hearts

Gaining popularity on Tumblr and Instagram, Light Academia has its roots in a love of knowledge. It celebrates the joy of learning, drawing inspiration from optimistic classics and philosophies that emphasize hope, motivation and gratitude. Works by authors such as Louisa May Alcott, Jane Austen and poets like Rumi resonate for their bright, uplifting ethos. The movement offers a space in which to appreciate idyllic moments in life, embodying a radiant, thankful approach to the pursuit of knowledge.

Dress code

Key elements of Light Academia include a pale and pastel color palette, vintage blouses, tailored pants and skirts, and knitted cardigans. Accessories often include classic books, delicate jewelry and vintage stationery.

Houndstooth jacket

Cable-knit sweater vest

Coin necklace

Collared blouse

Light-colored pants

Pleated short skirt

Crew socks

Loafers

Putting pen to paper

Journaling serves as both a creative outlet and a mindfulness practice. Fans of Light Academia often use vintage stationery to write down their reflections, poetry or scholarly notes.

Lovecore

Lovecore focuses on the aesthetics of romance, passion and affection, and expresses these sentiments via visual elements, activities and a general ethos of love.

⊕ Heart-shaped glasses

⊕ Love-themed hair clips

A return to romance

Emerging on platforms including Tumblr, Lovecore is a reaction to an increasingly cynical world. It serves as both a celebration of love and a form of rebellion against a society that stigmatizes emotional openness. Lovecore subculture is influenced by elements of vintage romance, classic fairy tales, and romantic scenes from popular culture. It invites people to unabashedly embrace love, promote positivity and inclusivity, and celebrate affection.

Puff sleeves

Heart-patterned clothing

Vintage-inspired skirt

Dress code

Lovecore is characterized by vibrant, often heart-themed, attire. Reds and pinks dominate the palette, along with heart patterns, lace and frills. Accessories often include heart-shaped jewelry, hair clips and bags.

Heart-shaped bag

Frilly socks

Red/pink shoes

Strawberries

Representing sweetness, innocence, and a touch of nostalgia, strawberry prints on dresses, skirts or tops are a delightful aspect of the Lovecore aesthetic.

Kidcore

Kidcore embraces the aesthetics, simplicity and joy of childhood. The term reflects the subculture's central theme of childlike innocence and an unbridled enthusiasm for life.

Escape to childhood

Emerging on Tumblr and TikTok, Kidcore—a nostalgic reflection and celebration of the aesthetics of '80s and '90s childhood—gained popularity among teenagers and young adults. It was seen as a response to the pressures of adulthood, and a space for people to reconnect with their inner child, find joy in simplicity, and express themselves without the constraints of societal expectations. Kidcore embodied a playful, carefree spirit, encouraging creativity, imagination and color.

Dress code

Kidcore clothing is characterized by vibrant colors, fun prints and playful accessories. Oversized T-shirts and overalls often feature cartoon characters, or rainbow and star motifs. Chunky plastic jewelry and children's backpacks complete the look.

Stuffed animals

From plush keychains attached to bags to large toys, stuffed animals are used as playful accessories.

Toy-like Jewelry

Rainbow clothing

Cartoon-print T-shirt

Overalls

Childlike motifs

Jelly shoes

Decorated shoelaces

Fashion, Fantasy & Futurism

Fashion, with its limitless room for imagination, serves as a powerful conduit for creating new worlds and realities. It's not only a dynamic reaction to societal shifts, but an expressive platform for individuality, enabling us to craft our own fantastical narratives.

A land of enchantment

By allowing people to fantasize about a magical realm full of mythical creatures, fashion provides a safe place for those who feel marginalized. It draws inspiration from both bright and shadowy imaginary worlds, allowing creativity to run wild.

Inspired by the past

Drawing from the beauty of the past, fashion weaves historical aesthetics into modern narratives. This exploration of our roots offers a reinvention of the old in novel and meaningful ways, marrying the past with the present.

Baroque era

Victorian era

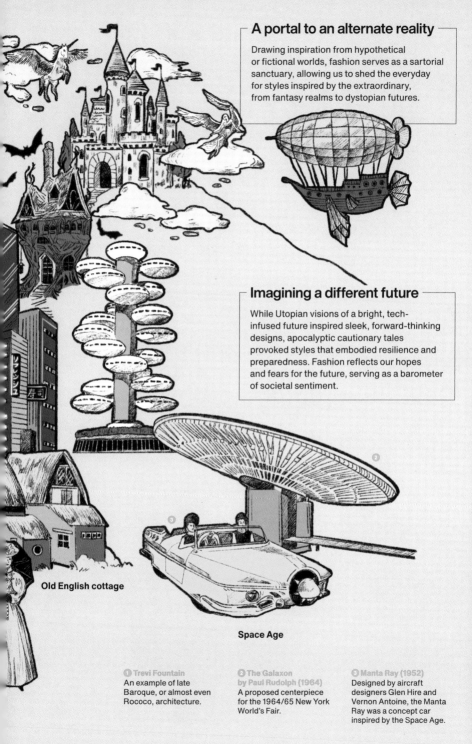

A portal to an alternate reality

Drawing inspiration from hypothetical or fictional worlds, fashion serves as a sartorial sanctuary, allowing us to shed the everyday for styles inspired by the extraordinary, from fantasy realms to dystopian futures.

Imagining a different future

While Utopian visions of a bright, tech-infused future inspired sleek, forward-thinking designs, apocalyptic cautionary tales provoked styles that embodied resilience and preparedness. Fashion reflects our hopes and fears for the future, serving as a barometer of societal sentiment.

Old English cottage

Space Age

1 Trevi Fountain
An example of late Baroque, or almost even Rococo, architecture.

2 The Galaxon by Paul Rudolph (1964)
A proposed centerpiece for the 1964/65 New York World's Fair.

3 Manta Ray (1952)
Designed by aircraft designers Glen Hire and Vernon Antoine, the Manta Ray was a concept car inspired by the Space Age.

Steampunk

Steampunk celebrates the technology and aesthetics of 19th-century steam-powered machinery. The term originated in the 1980s as a reference to Cyberpunk literature with an industrial, historic twist.

Sci-fi retro futurism

Originating as a subgenre of science fiction and fantasy, Steampunk was influenced by 19th-century scientific romances by writers including Jules Verne and H.G. Wells. Fans were inspired by the idea of advanced steam-powered technology existing in Victorian times. Steampunk reimagined historical fashion and technology using modern DIY craftsmanship. The subculture blends science fiction, history, fashion and technology into one retro-futuristic aesthetic style.

Dress code

Steampunk blends Victorian-era clothing with futuristic, mechanical elements. The palette is dark and sepia-toned, with metallic accents. Typical outfits include corsets, vests and goggles, often accentuated with gears, pocket watches and parasols.

❶ Top hat
This classic Victorian accessory is a staple of Steampunk fashion. They're often adorned with goggles, feathers or gears.

❷ Leather corset
A nod to Victorian fashion, corsets accentuate the silhouette and often feature leather or brocade.

❸ Bustle skirt
Inspired by late-Victorian fashion, these skirts add volume at the back using layers, ruffles or pleats. This vintage style is popular for its dramatic flair and feminine silhouette.

Frock coat

Victorian shirt

Fingerless gloves

Tailcoat

Victorian vest

High-waisted pants

4 Leather boots
Boots are often adorned with buckles, laces and metal detailing for an industrial look.

5 Pocket watch
An accessory indicative of the Victorian era's fascination with time and precision, pocket watches often feature ornate mechanical designs and are typically made of brass or copper.

6 Ray gun
Imaginative weapons, including ray guns and swords, are often used as accessories, inspired by the genre's science-fiction roots.

7 Gear jewelry
Gears are a common symbol of the industrial revolution; cuff links, necklaces and earrings often feature mechanical elements.

8 Parasol
These stylish Victorian accessories feature elements such as brass handles or lace detailing.

9 Goggles
A signature Steampunk accessory, old-fashioned goggles often feature brass frames, leather straps and tinted lenses. They're reminiscent of aviator or inventor eyewear.

Airship
This early innovation in aviation technology, invented in late 19th century, is associated with adventure and exploration.

Hair & make-up
Vintage-style make-up featured bold eyeliner, metallic touches, and dark, saturated lip colors. Victorian hair trends include updos, ringlets and hairpieces, often embellished with gears or other nods to the industrial aesthetic.

Wild Wild West (1999)
This steampunk action-comedy film, directed by Barry Sonnenfeld, follows two government agents as they investigate a diabolical genius who plans to use advanced technology to destabilize the United States.

Cyberpunk

Cyberpunk culture emerged in the 1980s,
inspired by science-fiction literature and films
depicting dystopian, technology-driven futures.

Reality meets virtual dystopia
Cyberpunk started as a literary
movement that explored the
consequences of technology.
Writers including William Gibson
and Bruce Sterling pioneered
the genre, exploring themes such
as a combination of low life and
high tech, and featuring gritty
urban settings juxtaposed with
futuristic technologies.
Their stories explored artificial
intelligence, virtual reality and
corporate domination. The
rebellious nature of the narratives
resonated with a growing
audience that identified with the
subculture's anti-establishment
ethos; this was fueled by
the internet and real-world
technological advances.

Dress code
Cyberpunk fashion is
characterized by dark, often
androgynous clothing including
leather jackets, futuristic
sunglasses, neon accents
and piercings. Hairstyles often
feature colorful locks and
shaved sides.

Blade Runner (1982)
This classic neo-noir
science-fiction film is set in
a dystopian Los Angeles.

Shaved
hair with
circuit-inspired
patterns

Neon
mohawk

Futuristic
jacket

Short
bomber
jacket

Face
piercing

Digital
gadgets

Fingerless
gloves

Leather
pants

Combat
boots

Cybergoth

Cybergoth combines Cyberpunk science fiction with Gothic fashion, adopting a futuristic look with a dystopian and apocalyptic edge.

Sci-fi Goth apocalypse

Cybergoth fashion originated as part of the wider Gothic rock and industrial music scenes in Europe in the late 1990s and early 2000s; it is a fusion of Goth, Cyberpunk and Rave-culture elements. The music, heavily influenced by electronic genres such as industrial and EBM (Electronic Body Music), explored themes of technology, transhumanism and dystopian futures. Cybergoth culture also drew inspiration from Cyberpunk literature and movies; this unique blend of influences allowed members to explore alternate identities.

Dress code

Cybergoth fashion is characterized by dark clothing with neon accents. Outfits often include PVC, leather or latex adorned with cyber-inspired accessories such as goggles, respirators and LED lights. Hair often features neon extensions and dreadlocks.

Goggles

Cyberlox

Respirator

Spiked collar

Sheer/ mesh top

Black pants

Fishnets/ torn mesh

Circuitry motif

Biohazard sign

Biohazard symbol

The biohazard symbol is often used in Cybergoth fashion. The symbol's association with danger and toxicity aligns with the Cybergoth fascination with dystopian and post-apocalyptic themes.

Fluffy leg warmers

Warcore

This burgeoning subculture fuses military and utilitarian aesthetics with streetwear, representing a lifestyle and an attitude that represents strength, resilience and a sense of individuality.

A show of strength

The Warcore subculture emerged as a response to global sociopolitical tensions and a desire for personal empowerment. Starting as an underground movement, it was fueled by social media and popularized by Gen Z and millennials. Warcore roots itself in the functionality and durability of military attire, which symbolizes preparedness and resilience; the combination of these elements with the edginess of streetwear creates a unique aesthetic. It emphasizes individual strength and adaptability, reflecting societal turbulence and the resolve to face it head-on.

Dress code

Warcore, as its name suggests, borrows heavily from military and survival gear including cargo pants, combat boots and tactical vests. Accessories include gas masks, goggles and chest rigs. Dark, muted tones dominate, with splashes of camo or neon for added edge.

Body armor
Military and motorcycle body armor is worn as a fashion statement.

Black cap

Face mask

Gas mask

Black hoodie

Utility vest

Cobra-buckle belt

Protective gloves

Combat boots

Camouflage

Black tech trainers

Avant Apocalypse

Avant Apocalypse emerged from a fascination with the end of the world and a desire to break free from traditional norms. The name means "before the apocalypse," and reflects a fascination with an uncertain, dystopian future.

Fashion for the end times

The Avant Apocalypse aesthetic is a response to an era rife with global crises, including climate change, epidemics, war and economic collapse. The subculture's adherents are often propelled by a sense of urgency, believing that humanity is on the brink of a cataclysmic event. This conviction has inspired a unique aesthetic that draws inspiration from a range of sources, including dystopian movies and high fashion, embracing deconstruction and repurposing old, damaged clothes into innovative new creations.

Dress code

Dramatic and unconventional, Avant Apocalypse outfits often incorporate deconstructed pieces, asymmetrical cuts and distressed fabrics. Exposed skin, bondage and knots are common elements. Dark, muted colors and metallic tones dominate the palette.

Goggles

Distressed finish

Strap elements

Deconstructed/ torn details

Military-style footwear

Rick Owens
American designer Rick Owens' unconventional silhouettes and distressed fabrics epitomize the subculture's dystopian, rebellious ethos.

Mad Max: Fury Road (2015)

Cottagecore

The Cottagecore aesthetic idealizes a simple, pastoral life. It's a nostalgic, romanticized interpretation of country living emphasizing self-sufficiency, sustainability and harmony with nature.

The simple life

Emerging on social media platforms around 2018, the trend gained popularity among urban millennials and Gen Z. Its rise is linked to the desire for a slower, more mindful life, away from the modern technology-driven hustle. Further fueled by pandemic-induced confinement at home, the trend's comforting imagery of rural tranquility helped people find solace. It was also seen as a subtle form of rebellion against consumerism and the fast-paced digital world, instead championing crafts, baking and gardening.

Dress code

Romantic, traditional rural style features flowy dresses, milkmaid tops and accessories made from natural materials, often with floral prints, lace or embroidery. Earth and pastel tones reflect the subculture's connection with nature.

❶ White lace dress
Lace is reminiscent of handcrafts and homemade goods, and white is usually associated with purity and simplicity.

❷ Wicker basket
Practical for picnics or foraging, wicker baskets are a nod to the past. Their natural material aligns with the subculture's emphasis on sustainability and tradition.

Headscarf

Smock dress

Peasant blouse

Low-heeled Oxfords

Floral crown

Hair bow

Lace-up boots

Mary Janes

Straw bag

High-waisted skirt

3 Straw hat
Often adorned with ribbons, wide-brimmed straw hats provide shade and a countryside vibe.

4 Prairie blouse
This 19th-century style—a feminine blouse with a high neckline and puff sleeves—is often adorned with lace or ruffle details, bringing to mind historical fashions.

5 Mushroom motif
Mushrooms and other motifs embroidered on handkerchiefs, blouses or textiles are popular for their homemade charm.

6 Milkmaid dress/top
This style—a loose, comfortable top with a square or sweetheart neckline, sometimes with smocking details—often has ruffles or puff sleeves. It is reminiscent of historical dress styles, evoking a romantic image.

7 Knitwear
Cozy, often oversized sweaters in soft neutrals channel *hygge* and crafting. Knitting is a traditional skill that fits into the slow lifestyle promoted by Cottagecore.

8 Quilted jacket
Quilting is a traditional craft that often mixes floral prints and colors; its aesthetic and its association with artisanship align with the values of the subculture.

Vintage furniture
Cottagecore embraces a slower, more mindful lifestyle. Its interior-design aesthetic often features vintage furniture, handmade decor and an abundance of houseplants. The look prioritizes sustainability, often repurposing antique items and embracing natural, rustic materials.

Moominvalley
Tove Jansson's Moomin series is set in an idyllic natural world. The Moomins' simple, nature-integrated lifestyle is filled with woodland adventures and familial bonds.

Baking is life
A quintessential Cottagecore activity, baking emphasizes homemade and wholesome food. Kneading dough, picking fresh berries for a pie and making fresh bread all embody self-sufficiency and finding joy in simple domestic tasks.

Angelcore

This niche subculture draws its name from a fascination with angelic and heavenly motifs. Its adherents embrace a serene ambience, embodying a celestial aura in their everyday lives and appearances.

The pursuit of purity

Angelcore found its footing on platforms such as Tumblr and Instagram, where users could share their inspirations and interpretations. The movement is tied closely to a longing for peace and tranquility, a reaction against the hectic pace of modern life. Its members are drawn to the idea of purity, innocence and benevolence—traditional hallmarks of angelic beings—which they strive to manifest in their personas and lifestyles.

Dress code

The overall aesthetic is soft and dreamy, with an emphasis on pastel and white clothing, flowing dresses, layers of lace and delicate fabrics. Jewelry often features wing, halo or cloud motifs.

Marcantonio Franceschini, *The Guardian Angel* (1716)

Divine inspiration

Angelcore draws inspiration from religious art, especially from the Renaissance and Baroque periods.

Halo-like headband

Angel wings

White, flowy dress

Frills

🔵 Gold & pearl jewelry

Witchcore

A subculture that infuses the aesthetic, mystical and spiritual elements of traditional witchcraft into modern fashion and lifestyle, Witchcore represents an eclectic blend of old-world charm and contemporary sensibilities.

Modern mysticism

Witchcore arose in the 2010s among young, digital-savvy individuals during a time of global uncertainty and sociopolitical shifts. It is often seen as a modern manifestation of ancient practices in which individuals seek comfort and empowerment from supernatural forces and nature. The aesthetic is heavily influenced by folk traditions, magic, herbalism and the allure of the occult. It reclaims the label "witch," which was once a mark of persecution; in Witchcore it means strength and independence.

Dress code

Witchcore fashion leans toward a dark, retro aesthetic. Key elements often include layered dresses, cloaks, lace and frills, usually black or in earth tones. Accessories often feature symbols of witchcraft, including pentagrams, moons, crystals and botanical motifs.

Wide-brimmed hat

Silver pentagram necklace

Lace top

Long black dress

Chiffon/ mesh layers

⬆ Sun & moon motif

⬆ Gris-gris
DIY bags filled with herbs, crystals and charms.

Facets of nature

Crystals are cherished for their reputed healing properties and connections to the earth's energy. Each one is believed to possess a different energy or benefit.

Victorian lace-up boots

Style Overview

012   014   015   016

Teen Power

040   042   044   046   048   050   052   053   054

The Swinging Sixties

058   060

The Neon Era

083   084   086   088   090

094   096   098   100   101   102

Alternative Goes Mainstream

130   132   134   136   137

140   142   144   145   146   148   150   152

176   178   180   182   184   185   186   188

Flash Fashion

192   194   196   198

Transformation Through War

| 018 | 020 | | 024 | 026 | 028 | 029 | | 030 | 032 | 033 | 034 | 036 |

Blossoming Revolution

| 062 | 064 | 066 | 068 | 069 | 070 | 072 | | 076 | 078 | 079 | 080 | 082 |

| 104 | 105 | 106 | 108 | 110 | 114 | 116 | 118 | 120 | 121 | 122 | 126 | 128 | 129 |

Dot-Com Era

| 156 | 157 | 158 | 160 | 162 | 163 | | 166 | 168 | 170 | 172 | 173 | 174 | 175 |

| 200 | 201 | 202 | 203 | 204 | 205 | 208 | 210 | 211 | 212 | 213 | 214 | 216 | 217 |

References

Books

100 Ideas that Changed Fashion
Harriet Worsley
Laurence King Publishing

Cool: Style, Sound, and Subversion
Greg Foley, Andrew Luecke
Rizzoli

Deadhead Social Science:
"You Ain't Gonna Learn What You Don't
Want to Know"
Rebecca G. Adams, Robert Sardiello
AltaMira Press

Fashion: The Definitive Visual Guide
(new edition)
DK, Smithsonian Institution
DK

Fashion Since 1900 (World of Art)
Amy de la Haye, Valerie Mendes
Thames & Hudson

Style and the Man
Alan Flusser
It Books

The Handbook of Style –
A Man's Guide to Looking Good
The editors of *Esquire*
Hearst Books/Sterling Publishing Co.

Out of the Box:
The Rise of Sneaker Culture
Elizabeth Semmelhack
Rizzoli Electa

Documentaries

Soul Train: The Hippest Trip in America
Amy Goldberg & J. Kevin Swain, 2010

The Hip Hop Years
David Upshal, 1999

China's Most Misunderstood Subculture
VICE Asia, 2014

Websites

471665674241657755.weebly.com
6dokidoki.com
80scasualclassics.co.uk
90sfashion.com
abc.net.au
aesthetics.fandom.com
anothermag.com
anyflip.com
apparelnetwork.it
archerytrade.org
artsandculture.google.com
askmen.com
attic.city
atwcweb.wordpress.com
audiblwav.com
bbc.com
belatina.com
bensonandclegg.com
beyondretro.com
bitrebels.com
blissgirl.com
blog.size.co.uk
bowties.com
briefly.co.za
britannica.com
buzzfeed.com
bygonely.com
byrdie.com
calibermag.net
centralcasting.com
chasingdaisiesblog.com
cheaney.co.uk
citizenside.com
classiq.me
clickamericana.com
complex.com
corbetosboots.com
core.ac.uk
cosmopolitan.com.hk
costumes.com.au
costumesociety.org.uk
counterculture.fandom.com
creativeboom.com
dailymail.co.uk
dallasobserver.com
dazeddigital.com
dbpedia.org
denimdudes.co
denofgeek.com
designmango.in
devilinspired.com
diggitmagazine.com

dispatch.com
dividingmoments.blogspot.com
dmarge.com
dreamstime.com
dubsnatch.com
edition.cnn.com
editorialist.com
electrowow.net
eleganceblog.com
enjoy-your-style.com
esquire.com
etsy.com
everywhereish.wordpress.com
faroutmagazine.co.uk
fashinnovation.nyc
fashion-era.com
fashion.mam-e.it
fashionablymale.net
fashionhistory.fitnyc.edu
fashionstudiesjournal.org
fidmmuseum.org
fieldstonnews.com
flashbacksummer.com
flashbak.com
fountainof30.com
gatamagazine.com
gentlemansgazette.com
gq.com
graduatestore.fr
grailed.com
grazia.co.in
grease.fandom.com
growbusniesshub.com
guycounseling.com
gyaru.fandom.com
haenfler.sites.grinnell.edu
hair-and-makeup-artist.com
harvard.edu
hausmeingott.com
heartafact.com
heddels.co
helenquinn.wordpress.com
highsnobiety.com
hipafrica.com
hiphopdance.fandom.com
hohohohoho.home.blog
huckmag.com
huffpost.com
humanitiescollaborative.utep.edu
hypebeast.com
i-d.vice.com
ideanow.online
idioteq.com
immaterieelerfgoed.nl

independent.co.uk
inlineskateworld.com
insider.com
instyle.com
interviewmagazine.com
invisibleoranges.com
ivy-style.com
juxtapoz.com
kcrw.com
koreascience.kr
leatherati.com
lofficielusa.com
lookiero.co.uk
lulus.com
luxurylondon.co.uk
magazine.sangbleu.com
majortests.com
martasubculturesproject.wordpress.com
masterclass.com
maytheray.com
mdig.com.br
medium.com
mens-folio.com
messynessychic.com
miabafrica.mondoblog.org
motherjones.com
museumofyouthculture.com
mymodernmet.com
new-rock-france.com
newportri.com
newtimeslo.com
nextshark.com
nicekicks.com
ninjacosmico.com
nme.com
nokillmag.com
nosetta.com
nytimes.com
okayafrica.com
openculture.com
orientdailynews.com
outsons.com
oystermag.com
per-spex.com
phoebepollittcontour.wordpress.com
piledriverz.com
popsugar.com
potentash.com
prologue.blogs.archives.gov
punkabilly-clothing.com
punkjourney.com
qz.com
raleighvintage.com
ravenfoxcapes.com

read01.com
rebelsmarket.com
reddit.com
refinery29.com
retropond.com
retrowaste.com
returnofthecaferacers.com
reuters.com
rollerskatedad.com
rosashoes.com
rustyzipper.com
saigoneer.com
sammydvintage.com
sartorialscholars.wordpress.com
scene.fandom.com
sciencedirect.com
scramblerworld.wordpress.com
seattlemet.com
skooldays.com
sndct.com
sportshistoryweekly.com
stylesofman.com
subcultureslist.com
suemtravels.com
superprof.com
surfer.com
tatlerasia.com
tdpclothing.tattoo
techwear-outfits.com
techwholesale.com
the-comm.online
theavenuemag.com
thebrightestbrunette.com
thecut.com
thedailybeast.com
thefader.com
thefashionwolf.com
thefemin.com
theglobeandmail.com
theguardian.com
thejapaneseshop.co.uk
thelexingtonline.com
themadameblue.com
themoodguide.com
theolympians.co
theriotgrrrlproject.tumblr.com
thesolesupplier.co.uk
thetimes.co.uk
thetrendspotter.net
thevou.com
thezoereport.com
thisisdig.com
throttlesnake.com
ties.com
timeslive.co.za
tiviakiblog.wordpress.com
travelnoire.com
tvtropes.org
tweedlandthegentlemansclub.blogspot.com

underground-england.com
unframed.lacma.org
urbandictionary.com
utopiast.com
vam.ac.uk
vanityfair.it
vassar.edu
vervemagazine.co.nz
vice.com
vintag.es
vintage-retro.com
vintagedancer.com
vintagehairstyling.com
vintageinn.ca
vintagemaedchen.de
vintagenewsdaily.com
virtualjapan.com
vocal.media
vogue.co.uk
vogue.com
vogue.fr
vogue.it
voguescandinavia.com
vox.com
voxfrock.com.au
washingtonpost.com
webringjustice.wordpress.com
wefashiontrends.com
who.com.au
whowhatwear.com
wikihow-fun.com
wikihow.com
wikipedia.org
williams.edu
wise-geek.com
witness2fashion.wordpress.com
wmagazine.com
womens-fashion.lovetoknow.com
worldcrunch.com
wsj.com
ww2incolor.com
wwdjapan.com
youtube.com
zani.co.uk

Acknowledgements

Chairman
Penter Yip

Editor in Chief
Ronnie Tung

Editors
Sara Chow
Mango Leung

Designer
Toby Ng Design

Illustrators
Vikki Yau
Selina Chuk
Kiki Yuen
Chuyi Lai

Copy Editor
Lisa Burnett Hillman

Contributors
Eva Pong
Mildred Lo
Candice Lam
Juliana Hui